# MONSTERLAND:
## Encounters with UFOS, Bigfoot and Orange Orbs

## RONNY LE BLANC

# DEDICATION

This book is dedicated to my sister Cara Le Blanc Kelly who always wanted to write a book but passed away from cancer at such a young age, my mother Katherine Le Blanc who has continued to encourage me in all of my creative endeavors and pushed me to write this book. My father, Ron Le Blanc Sr., my life adviser, who is always persuading me to continue to learn and to follow my passions in life, and my beautiful and patient wife Amy Le Blanc who has had to deal with my lifelong obsession firsthand. Thank you for putting up with me!

# CONTENTS

RONNY LE BLANC

# ACKNOWLEDGMENTS

Thank you to my friends and fellow truth seekers, Susan McNeill-Spuhler and Willy Miranda for allowing me to speak and be a part of the New England UFO Conference in 2015 and 2016. It created a deadline and it drove me to complete this book. Thank you to Mike Paterson for allowing me to interview you for the book and to use your photos.

Thank you to the Leominster Public Library for putting up with me and my endless requests for books from across the state of Massachusetts. When the book titles came in, they knew who they were going to.

To my Editor in life and the Editor of this book, my best friend and my smoking hot wife Amy Le Blanc, Thank you sweetness! I couldn't have done it without you!

# 1

# MONSTERLAND, MASSACHUSETTS

I was born and raised in Leominster, Massachusetts. After graduating Leominster High School I headed west for college in Southern California. I attended Vanguard University in Costa Mesa studying film and television production, graduating with a degree in Communications. I spent almost a decade on the west coast living in Los Angeles working in the entertainment industry. I am a musician, an artist and I love the outdoors. I grew up in a Christian home.

We attended church every Sunday and I also went to a youth group where I met some of the best people, some of whom are friends to this day. The time spent there and with these great people, really forged my character and perception of life and what our purpose here is all about. However, even though I attended church and tried to follow the straight and narrow, I do not consider myself a religious person.

I consider myself to be spiritual and I believe in karma. What you put out into the universe comes back to you. I am what some consider a "truth seeker". I have often wondered where we truly came from and where we are headed when we die. I have been fascinated with consciousness, science, space and strange stories that have been echoed for eons. I am an inquisitive person and I have always questioned the unkonwn. If God made us, who made God? While I was in California I started to study Zen Buddhism and Eastern philosophy. I have had some strange things happen to me while growing up in Leominster, when I moved back home they continued. I have always felt that there was something different and special about the city I grew up in.

I was riding my bike one summer day on the trails behind Fall Brook School and headed into what is known as MONSTERLAND. I had always avoided a particular trail along the way to the sand pits where kids would ride their four-wheelers and dirt bikes. For a twelve-year-old alone in the woods, I always felt an eerie feeling when I was anywhere near this trail. It was a feeling mixed with dread and fear.

It didn't matter if it was a cloudless day the opening of the trail and the woods deep inside seemed to be covered in darkness and haunted fog. It was guarded by two large oak trees on either side. This created an unwelcoming prehistoric looking gate for those tempted to explore any further. In my imagination, I could see coyotes and bears just waiting to pounce on me. But on this day, I was feeling incredibly daring and decided to brave the trail.

The trail itself had a decent incline. I had to jump off my bike and walk it in. As I made my way along, I couldn't shake the fear that increased with every step. I kept looking behind me, feeling something or someone's gaze. After a few yards, the terrain was a little easier to manage, and I got back on my bike and slowly started to pedal forward. The pedals squeaked with each rotation. Nervous, I scanned around me. My senses were on high alert. I don't know what possessed me to do so, but I stopped. With both of my feet planted firmly on the ground, balancing the bike between my legs, I listened. Nothing. Dead quiet. There were no birds chirping and singing. There were no squirrels scurrying along the ground. I wondered where all the animal life had disappeared to?

I looked straight ahead as the trail narrowed. I wanted to start pedaling again, but it was as if I hit a mental wall. I couldn't convince myself to move forward. The trees had created a high canopy and there were solid rays of sunlight ripping through the gaps of space between the leaves, lighting only select parts of the forest floor. Mesmerized, I watched the opposing shadows as they seemed to playfully dance along in front of me.

The silence quickly evaporated when only a few yards away, I heard something crash through the woods so loudly and with such force, that I felt it in my chest. I literally shook. Up through the soles of my feet, the sounds of the footsteps reverberated through my body. It sounded like it was something very large and my mind equated it to an elephant stomping away at a sprint.

My eyes were fixated on the sea of green ferns, grasses, and small trees violently being pushed aside. I couldn't see anything making its path through the forest. My adrenaline pumped so hard, I thought that my heart might punch a hole through my chest. It was as if I was frozen in place until I couldn't hear the sounds anymore because suddenly, I snapped out of my zombie-like state. I felt like I could move again. Gathering my wits, I slammed my butt back onto my bike and headed back home as fast as I could. I don't think I have pedaled a bike faster in my life.

On the way home my brain was racing, trying to comprehend what had just happened. What did I just encounter? It didn't make any sense at all. But I told myself that it didn't matter what it was. I would not be going back. I never ventured down that trail again.

As I got older, I realized I had totally forgotten about what happened to me in those woods. The memory resurfaced again as I started to look into the stories of Bigfoot in this area, thirty years later. Looking back, I wonder if I had a Bigfoot encounter at the early age of twelve. It was something.

MONSTERLAND. It is situated in an unlikely place. It lies in the southern part of Leominster, bordering the neighboring town of Lancaster, in central Massachusetts. It never dawned on me how this particular piece of land got its name. Monsterland is a location where people have reportedly gone missing in connection to being in contact with a monster, better known the world over as Bigfoot or Sasquatch.

In legendary cryptozoologist and author Loren Coleman's book, *Monsters of Massachusetts*, published in 2013, he wrote the following about Leominster State Forest and Monsterland:

*Another site of importance is the Leominster State Forest, a 4,300-acre parcel of forested land that includes the Wachusett Mountain State Reservation, containing the largest known area of old-growth forest east of the Connecticut River in Massachusetts. The entire greenway is composed of hardwood forests, alpine meadows, ponds, streams, and wood shrub swamps. The area supports a rich and diverse wildlife and bird population.*

*Findings of Bigfoot tracks are so frequent in the area of Southern Leominster that it is known by residents thereabouts as "MONSTERLAND," a name that began during the time of sightings by local citizens of a hairy manlike creature off Route 2 in the 1950's and 1960's. (1)*

The stories go back almost a century. In 1884, a hunter witnessed some type of beast or creature while it walked upright and then once it was spotted, it dropped down and it broke out into a sprint using all fours. That same year, a local farmer claimed that he watched helplessly as a creature tore his cattle to shreds then ran off into the woods...on two legs.

According to *StrangeUSA.com*, legend has it that sometime on a summer evening in the 1950's, a man abruptly enters a local bar in Leominster. He excitedly tells the manager of the establishment that he just witnessed a "terrifying monster" by the bridge on Old Mill Road. Long before cell phones would be ubiquitous and at everyone's fingertips, he asks the manager to call the police. The manager, who had taken the man seriously, sensing the fear in the stranger's eyes, obliges and calls the Leominster Police Station.

After waiting for a short period of time, the visibly shaken man tells the manager of the bar that he is tired of waiting for the police, time is wasting. He states that he is going to go back and kill the creature. "I am going to prove to everyone that this thing is real!" He leaves the bar and heads back to where he last saw the beast near the bridge.

When the police finally arrive at the bar, which appears to be located at the now named bar called Miranda's on Lancaster Street, the man making the amazing claim of seeing a monster is now gone. The manager then quickly explains to the police officers the frightened man's plan of heading back to the bridge in pursuit of the mysterious beast.

The officers head over to Old Mill Road hoping to find him. They arrive only to find his empty vehicle on the west side of the bridge, with its lights on. The police, expecting he would eventually return to his car, decided to wait. When he never emerges from the woods, the officers then conduct a search of the area. He was never found.

Two hunters several years ago were hunting in the woods behind the Sholan Farms area of Leominster. They found two deer carcasses hanging up in an apple tree near their hunting area. They looked like they were partially eaten and the hunters assumed that it was the work of a mountain lion. But the Eastern Mountain Lion isn't supposed to exist. I found it curious that there was no other explanation for what other animal could have done this. The hunters were so freaked out by what they saw they immediately left the area. I began to wonder if someone or "something" might be trying to tell them to "stay away?"

The apple orchard where these carcasses were discovered sits between Fall Brook and Heyward Reservoirs (Monsterland) with a straight shot west through some swamp and into Leominster State Forest. The same area where six five-toed human-like footprints were found in 2010.

Sasquatch have been known to use trees as markers, bending down the limbs, weaving them together or breaking off branches higher than any animal could reach, even a moose. Hunters are said to have found trees shredded apart in Leominster State Forest. When others have asked the hunters if they thought that it might be a moose or deer doing this, they replied that "If it was either a moose or deer, they wouldn't want to meet it. It would have to have the power of a backhoe to do what we saw." (2)

Due to the small amount of Bigfoot sightings that are reported on several Bigfoot websites for central Massachusetts (BFRO shows that there are twenty-six total for Massachusetts and only four in Worcester County, Leominster with one), it would seem to anyone by the sheer lack of numbers that Massachusetts and the area in and around Leominster wouldn't be considered a Bigfoot "Hotspot". (3)

I recently spoke with Jonathan Wilk, who is the lead investigator of the Massachusetts chapter of the Bigfoot Field Researchers Organization (BFRO), who stated that they have over one hundred open cases of Bigfoot sightings and reports that have yet to be followed up on within the great state of Massachusetts. Jonathan told me that they get reports from Monsterland and the surrounding areas all the time.

For a majority of the people that reside in North America, most know only of the legend of Bigfoot and that it falls into the category of the imagination and folklore, like dragons, fairies, and leprechauns. The general consensus it seems is that the "kind of people" who see Sasquatch in the woods when they are hiking or witness a UFO hovering above a field are considered somehow mentally challenged, or that they were "on something". Bigfoot isn't real. It's a myth.

There has yet to be a Bigfoot body to surface from the depths of mythology and legend to make this animal come to life for the rest of the world to see and believe. Some people that do believe in Bigfoot or Sasquatch, believe that it is an undiscovered primate yet to be classified by science.

The late Washington State University anthropologist Dr. Grover Krantz and Dr. John Bindernagel, a wildlife biologist from Canada, were convinced that Bigfoot is a relative of the giant ape, *Gigantopithecus Blacki*, which roamed the areas of China, India, and Vietnam some 200,000 years ago. Dr. John Bindernagel also believes that the Bigfoot sightings in the eastern states are just as convincing as those in the more well-known Pacific Northwest. "*I realized that the deciduous (season* trees) forest of the East are in many ways richer in life than the coniferous (evergreen) forests in the West, and that could sustain a large ape." (4)

Others believe that it could be a race of ancient humans, undiscovered and behind us on the evolutionary chain. With healthy populations across North America due to the thousands of sightings, photos, videos, footprint casts and hair samples found, it seems illogical that they would remain undiscovered.

These sightings can't all be explained away as hoaxes. There are 3,313 *reported* sightings across the United States and Canada over the course of 92 years, between 1920 and 2013. (5) The BFRO database has over 12,000!

What needs to be addressed is the fact that there are an unknown amount of sightings that are never reported due to the fear of being ridiculed by others and getting yourself labeled as "crazy". So if that is the case, that there are a majority of Bigfoot experiences and sightings that go unreported every year, that number could be tenfold.

Leominster State Forest, another area that seems to have a lot of unusual activity, encompasses the following surrounding five towns: Westminster, Princeton, Leominster, Fitchburg, and Sterling. The forest has a rich history of land use, dating back to Native Americans who used the Crow Hill ledges for shelter and for sending smoke signals to neighboring tribes.

Leominster was originally inhabited by various divisions of the Pennacook or Nipmuc Native Americans, who lived along the Nashua River. The Nashaway (or Nashua or Weshacum) were a tribe of Algonquian Indians inhabiting the upstream portions of the Nashua River valley in what is now the northern half of Worcester County, Massachusetts, mainly in the vicinity of Sterling, Lancaster and other towns near Mount Wachusett.

In the early 1700's, a series of land grants were given to the heirs of soldiers killed in the French and Indian Wars, by the General Court of Massachusetts Bay Colony. Many of these parcels became part of the unincorporated settlement known as Notown, almost all of which is part of Leominster State Forest today.

Due to its isolation from neighboring communities to thrive, it ceased to exist. In 1838 the lands of Notown were incorporated into the towns of Leominster, Fitchburg, Westminster, and Princeton. Today, there are still numerous root cellar holes, stone walls and curiously placed stone structures visible along the forest roads and trails. (6)

One of those trails that runs through the State Forest is the mid-state trail. This trail runs for 92 miles from Rhode Island to New Hampshire. The trail passes through the western edge of Leominster State Forest and includes the summits of Mount Wachusett and Mount Watatic. Animals follow and use these trails consistently, as well as power line routes and other game trails. Bigfoot has been theorized to do the same.

I have always had an interest in Bigfoot, UFOs and the paranormal. These are some of the biggest mysteries of the universe and I have always wanted to know the truth. The idea of the unexplainable has always fascinated me. I have spent a lot of time reading books and researching and as such, I have become sort of a resource for these types of experiences or encounters amongst friends who will often reach out to me with their stories as well as the experiences of others.

If there is something living in the Leominster woods, and if the stories are true; then one would have to assume that this isn't the same creature that people are seeing around here in the present day that they saw back then there would have to be more than one.

One would think that there would be more sightings of these creatures, but most people when they go hiking or biking stay on the trail. Rarely do people go "off trail", as this is a quick way to get lost in the woods. The forest is so thick during the summer months that one can barely see about four feet in front of them. You are surrounded by green leaves and endless trees and certain areas are difficult to traverse through with the overgrowth.

Many UFO and Bigfoot researchers, including myself, have suggested that the Bigfoot and UFO phenomena are connected; due to the fact that they are seen together and often appearing in the same areas year after year.

These theories haven't been accepted with open arms, but it is worth a look. I started to not only explore the Bigfoot stories and its history in Massachusetts but then discovered that there was a strong correlation with the UFOs that have been seen in the Bay State. UFOs also seem to be a part of Leominster's somewhat hidden and untold history. I started with researching Leominster and Worcester County and then spanned out to the borders of the state. My goal is to compile as many of the different stories about UFOS, Bigfoot, and other strange phenomena and see how they may be intertwined.

The late Harvard psychiatrist Dr. John E. Mack who won a Pulitzer Prize for his book on the alien abduction phenomenon came to the conclusion that there was a connection between all types of paranormal activity.

*"Taken together, these phenomena tell us many things about ourselves and the universe that challenge the dominant materialist paradigm. They reveal that our understanding of reality is extremely limited, the cosmos is more mysterious than*

*we have imagined, that there are other intelligences all about, some of which seem able to reach us. Consciousness itself may be the primary creative force of the universe, and our knowledge of the physical properties of this world is far from complete. The emerging picture is a cosmos that is an interconnected harmonic web, vibrating with creativity and intelligence, in which separateness is an illusion." (7)*

Not only do I feel that the Bigfoot and UFO phenomena are connected, there is also the element of synchronicity that seems to envelop the mystery. Synchronicity is a concept, first explained by psychiatrist Carl Jung, which holds that events are "meaningful coincidences" if they occur with no causal relationship, yet seem to be meaningfully related. For example, you think of a coyote and then a few seconds later out of the blue, a coyote crosses the road in front of you as you are driving down the road. When it occurs, there is this unknown "knowing" that the events are somehow interconnected. At times, it also seems as if the events themselves are orchestrated by some higher power. Some of these experiences and observations will amaze you and scare you at the same time. Everything happens for a reason.

For my role as Director of Digital Advertising for the Boston Herald, I would travel quite frequently to meet with clients and agencies nationwide. In the spring of 2013, I had a bunch of agency meetings in Manhattan that spanned a couple of days. Wearing a suit and tie, I would normally have one of my sales representatives with me. But for this particular trip, I was solo. When I would travel, I would always seek out any bookstores, big or small. I ended up having some time to spare in between meetings and I decided to check out the Borders Bookstore next to Madison Square Garden. I went straight to the "New Age" section where books about UFOs, Bigfoot, and Ghosts are categorized under.

With my head tilted to the side, I slowly scanned the book titles looking for anything on Bigfoot or UFOs that I hadn't devoured yet. I suddenly had the feeling like someone was watching me. That's when I noticed this lady, a brunette, wearing all black and in her early fifties, looking in my direction.

I continued to browse through the books and I could still feel her gaze even with my back turned to her. She then slowly made her way over to me and was now looking at the same section of books. We were literally standing right next to each other, maybe a foot away. I looked over again at her. She was now completely turned and staring right at me. "I am sorry", she said. "I noticed that you were looking at the books about UFOs?"

"Yes, I have been into UFOs, Bigfoot and the paranormal ever since I was a child." She then quickly says "You realize that most of this stuff is crap right? There are some good ones but more bad than good." I nodded and said, "Yes, I have read some of the bad, but the good ones have really opened my eyes."

"You have a very strong aura," she told me. "I noticed it right away. It's crystal clear. Very rare to see one like yours. Mine is clear as well. I am a witch. Do you realize that 'they' look for people like us?" I had a lump in my throat. "Who looks for people like us?" I questioned. She then looked up to the ceiling as if the answer was in the sky. "They are able to locate people like us, we have a higher vibration. There is a big change coming. Why do you think you are so interested in UFOs? Do you think that you have been taken?"

I thought about it for a second. "Oh boy, I don't think so. I have had some interesting experiences growing up, though. I went to school for filmmaking and screenwriting in Southern California. I have read so much about the subject, I figure I will write a movie about this stuff," I confidently replied. She paused for a moment and just stared at me. She then smiled, as if someone was telling her something, she listened intently and then took a breath and said "You are right. You are going to write something. But it's not going to be a movie, though. It's going to be a book and it's going to change the way people think about all of this. It's going to help pave the way for a change. But it won't be for a couple of years from now. You aren't ready yet."

I just stared back at her in disbelief. "I don't know about that, I have no desire to write a book," I said firmly. She responded, "You will, in time." Feeling uncomfortable about the conversation, I abruptly pulled out my phone and looked at the clock.

My meeting was in twenty minutes. I told her it was great talking with her and wished her well, but I had to go, otherwise I was going to be late for my meeting. I politely said "Goodbye". I walked away shaking my head, thinking about how absurd her comment was about me writing a book. That would never happen.

# 2

# LEOMINSTER AND UFOS

Leominster is known as the "Pioneer Plastics City" for its part in shaping the plastics industry. It garnered the nickname of "Comb City" due to its production of plastic combs, thanks to the invention of celluloid and the development of injection molding. Products like Foster Grant sunglasses, Tupperware and the Pink Flamingo, which have adorned lawns across America, were born in Leominster.

The very first European settlers began arriving in the mid-17th century and in 1653, the area of Leominster was first founded as part of the town of Lancaster. In the year 1675, the King Philips War started and took the lives of hundreds of people. In order to avoid further conflict with the native Indians, the settlers negotiated with Chief Sholan, the Sachem of the Nashaway tribe for the land. It would be the only parcel of land to be legally purchased in Central Massachusetts. The town of Leominster was officially established on July 4th, 1740. (8)

The city of Leominster was also an integral part of the Underground Railroad that ushered slaves from the south up into Canada. Leominster was a major stop along the way. The Emory Stearn Schoolhouse and the Francis Drake and Jonathan Drake house led anti-slavery campaigns and helped house

14

fugitive slaves. A disguised Fredrick Douglas stayed in Leominster for two weeks, when he was a wanted slave at the time. Rumor has it that Douglas sharpened his skills learning how to write and read while staying here. He went on to become a National abolitionist leader, an orator and a statesman.

Leominster is also known as being the birthplace of our biggest celebrity, John Chapman, otherwise known worldwide as Johnny Appleseed. He was a nurseryman who introduced apples to many of the states along the east coast, eventually becoming an American Legend. Disney would make an animated movie about him in 1948.

The city was also the center of a "Time Traveler" video several years ago that went viral on social media. It's known as the "Time Traveling Mobile Phone Footage from 1938." There is black and white film footage of a woman by the name of Gertrude Jones who is speaking on what looks like a mobile telephone.

It is purportedly a pre-war prototype of a wireless phone device developed by a communications factory owned by Dupont in Leominster. Gertrude's grandson going by the username "Planetcheck" said that the girl in the film is his grandmother. He states that he asked her about it and she remembers it well.

Gertrude was one of five women that were given this phone prototype to test out for a week. She was talking to one of the scientists who was holding another wireless phone and is off to the right of Gertrude when she walks into the frame of the film. (9)

The film is still included as an example of a "time traveler" using a cell phone, something that would not be invented until

1973. It would eventually be created thirty-five years later by Martin Cooper, an executive with Motorola. The first cell phone was called the Motorola DynaTAC.

Unbeknownst to some, Leominster is also known as a UFO hotspot. That's probably why The Greater New England UFO Conference was started and is held at City Hall in Leominster every October. Steve Firmani, a Leominster resident, was the former New England Director of MUFON, (The Mutual UFO Network). MUFON is the world's oldest and largest UFO phenomenon investigative organization.

Steve Firmani is also the founding father of the New England UFO Conference. The new organizers Willy Miranda and Susan McNeill-Spuhler both have had their own UFO experiences in Leominster. When Susan was in the womb, her mother told her that there was a cigar-shaped UFO with windows hovering above their home on West Street. Willy's mother and brother, while they were walking in downtown Leominster on a sunny, summer day watched a saucer-shaped UFO as it hovered over city hall in the late 1990's. Watching it until it shot away at a great speed.

There was also purportedly a UFO landing as well. Several years ago, there were sightings of a craft in the area. It seemed to have landed and a Leominster resident investigated the scene the next day and located tripod or landing gear indentations on the ground. The sand around the area of the landing showed signs of vitrification. This is when sand is heated up to the point where its existing matter is transformed into glass.

The Rendlesham Forest Incident, which is known as the "British Roswell", is probably one of the best documented UFO cases in the world. It was a case that involved the United States

Air Force personnel and security police. The Rendlesham Forest incident was a UFO encounter over the course of three nights in 1980 on the joint RAF Bentwaters and RAF Woodbridge bases in the United Kingdom. They were twin NATO bases, where a craft landed in the forest adjacent to the bases. Several soldiers were within feet of the landed craft. Symbols and writing like hieroglyphics were found on the outside of the craft. It is rumored that the base housed nuclear warheads and the craft was seen hovering over the munitions area.

One of those police officers on the base that was involved in this historic UFO event was Steve LaPlume, a Leominster native. LaPlume observed the craft fly right over him while he was on duty. He shared his story for the first time, speaking only once in thirty years at the New England UFO conference in 2014. He said he will never speak about it again. A bit of his story is included in the book *Left at East Gate* co-written by Peter Robbins and Larry Warren. Larry was one of the military police officers involved in the case.

There was a multitude of UFO sightings during the years of 1966-68 in Massachusetts. The Central Massachusetts area seemed to be a magnet for UFOs specifically in the year 1967. In the book, *The Andreasson Affair* by UFO investigator Raymond E. Fowler, the author points to the significance of the surrounding UFO sightings in the area and their interest in freshwater ponds, he states:

> *"Significantly, a great number of 1967 UFO reports involved sightings in upper central Massachusetts. A number of reports of objects hovering over freshwater ponds came from Phillipston, Royalston, Orange, and Tully, Massachusetts."* (10)

Famed alien abductee Betty Andreasson, had her first

extraterrestrial encounter while living in Leominster when she was a young girl. Her most notable and incredible abduction encounter, which included her family being frozen in suspended animation as well as exploring a UFO craft and interacting with its occupants, occurred in South Ashburnham on January 25th, 1967. Her story was the subject of five different books by Raymond E. Fowler. An investigation team was put together which included a solar physicist, an aerospace engineer, an electronics engineer, a hypnotist, a medical doctor, a telecommunications specialist and a UFO investigator.

She had fourteen sessions of regression hypnosis, two lie-detector tests, a psychiatric review and a character reference check. Both Betty and her daughter Becky had experienced UFOs and encounters with the typical grey aliens. The results of the inquiry would eventually be published in a 528-page account that stated that they were both sane individuals, both agreed upon the details of the encounters and that they had experienced something that they believed to be otherworldly. The 1972 PSE analysis report on both Betty Andreasson and her daughter Becky concluded, "They were telling the truth with regards to the 1967 incident...In the opinion of this analyst, the results are conclusive. (11)

During the course of the investigation and afterward, Betty and her husband Bob Luca were placed under FBI surveillance, had their phones tapped and had low flying unmarked black helicopters buzzing over their property. Author Raymond E. Fowler confirmed that Betty's family had "men in black" watching their house and black unmarked helicopters hovering over their home! (12)

On March 25th, 1980, while Betty was placed under hypnosis, she relived a UFO experience at the age of seven that occurred in Leominster, Massachusetts. The year was 1944 and while Betty was in her playhouse waiting for her girlfriend, a bright marble-shaped object flew in and affixed itself to Betty's temple. She grew faint and then she heard a voice in her head.

The voice told her that *"They have been watching me...I'm coming along fine...good progress...I was going to be happy very soon...Other people were going to be happy...getting some things ready to show me...It wouldn't be until I was twelve."* (13)

While walking in the woods in Westminster, Betty would encounter a grey alien, wearing a strange suit. Seconds later, a glowing ball of light was released from the alien's suit. In a similar fashion like the occurrence in Leominster, the orb attached itself to Betty's temple. It delivered another message through a voice in her head. The voice explained that she has still another year. They are preparing the path of the future so that she may help others.

This glowing ball also made an appearance during the 1980 hypnosis sessions. Betty saw an alien in the room "fade in and then fade out" before the ball of light showed up. One of the team members who was a police officer witnessed the ball of light resting on the curtain, almost as if it was watching the hypnosis session.

Raymond Fowler in one of his books entitled *The Watchers*, talks specifically about the year 1967 and UFOs in and around the cities surrounding Leominster and South Ashburnham:

> *The Condon Report may have dismissed UFOs but the UFOs were not listening. The year 1967 brought scores of unexplained reports to my attention as Massachusetts Director of a Subcommittee for the National Investigations Committee on Aerial Phenomena (NICAP). At that time I did not have the vaguest notion of Betty's abduction from her home at*

*South Ashburnham. However, there were many sightings all around the perimeter of her hometown. Many of the domed disks and cylindrical objects observed at close range cause electrical interference with automobile ignition systems, radios, and television, and even area power failures.*

*A former Coast Guard pilot and owner of a small airport, awakened by a humming sound, went outside to be confronted by a domed disk manned by two small humanoid figures.*

*Towns all around Betty's hometown reported oval objects hovering over freshwater ponds in the area. In the adjoining town of Leominster, a wife watched helplessly as a hovering oval object paralyzed and pinned her husband to the outside frame of their car. Just one week before this occurred, Betty Andreasson was abducted from the adjoining town of South Ashburnham.* (14)

The UFO case that Fowler references occurred at St. Leo's Cemetery, which is down the street from Betty Andreasson's first experience with the UFO phenomenon. She was living on Howard Street in Leominster, two streets over.

The Leominster Police investigated the incident. They quickly discovered that the witnesses were truly shaken up. The investigating officer explained that they had experienced something real and according to his expertise...they were telling the truth.

Incredibly, another street over, on that same stretch of road, lies the pub, now called Miranda's. Miranda's was the scene of our missing man in Leominster that we discussed in Chapter one who charged into the bar, described a hairy beast that he courageously went back for, but never returned to tell the tale during in the 1950's.

St. Leo's cemetery is right down the street from where I currently reside in Leominster. I jog by the "scene of the crime" in the morning during my daily running routine and always marvel that this space had a craft with extraterrestrials visiting Leominster several years back.

The Leominster Police Department was called to the scene and Lieutenant Matteo Ciccone interrogated the couple until 4:30 AM. He knew the family very well and he felt that they had experienced something real. William was known by the officer as well as his mother as not being afraid of anything. This was labeled one of the unknown UFO incidents and it happened in Leominster.

In *UFO Testament: Anatomy of an Abductee*, author Raymond Fowler shares this tale of the Flying saucer encounter in Leominster:

> *"According to the US Weather service, March 8th, 1967, was a clear, cool night. Visibility was twelve miles. In Boston, the thermometers read 28 degrees F. A recent snowstorm had left a beautiful blanket of white velvet draped over the fields and trees. A couple I'll call Mr. and Mrs. William Roberts of Leominster, Massachusetts, got a sudden inspiration to go for a late night scenic drive through the countryside. After driving for an hour and a half, they started home.*
>
> *At about 1:00 AM, they entered the town of Leominster where, as Mrs. Roberts later told investigator Frank Pechulis, "We suddenly came across a very thick fog and had to slow our car to a real low speed for safety reasons."*

"As we passed the cemetery," Mr. Roberts continued, "I noticed what looked like a large light to my left. I asked my wife if she saw anything, and she said no. I was certain that I had and decided I would look again." Mr. Roberts thinking that the light might be a fire and the fog was smoke, turned his car around and drove back into the mist. This time, they both saw the light. The bright glow was not from a fire, but from an object glowing in the air directly above the cemetery! At this point, Mr. Roberts lowered his window and excitedly told his wife, "I think we have something here!"

He parked his car broadside to the hovering object, which hung in the air a bare two hundred yards away. Bright as an acetylene torch, it was shaped like a flattened egg and emitted a sound like a dynamo.

Against his wife's wishes, William got out of the car. Excitedly, he raised his hand and pointed it at the blazing object. Simultaneously, the automobile lights, radio, and engine ceased functioning. At the same time, Mr. Roberts received an electrical shock. Almost instantaneously, his body became numb and immobilized from head to foot, and his arm was thrust back against the car by some unseen force, hitting the roof so hard that an imprint was made in the ice and snow.

"When the car went dead," Mrs. Roberts interjected, "I was yelling for Bill to get back in the car, but he did not move."

"I was unable to move," Mr. Roberts told the investigator. "My wife was in a panic. My mind was not at all affected. I just couldn't move!"

*When he did not respond to her screams, she slid across the seat and tugged at his jacket through the open window. He could hear her begging him to come back inside, but couldn't move a muscle. He was totally paralyzed from head to foot.*

*Mr. Roberts recalled, "I was there thirty to forty seconds before the object moved away. It moved quickly at an ever-increasing speed, not instantly." Abruptly, their car's lights and radio came back on. The humming object had accelerated upward and out of sight above the dense fog patch.*

*(On the following day in Andover, Massachusetts, witnesses would sight a strangely-lit silent object hovering about one thousand feet above the grounds of a country club.) (15)*

I was told a story that there was a UFO sighting along Main Street in Leominster, during the 1980's. There were several boys, fourteen to fifteen years old, who were walking home late at night from their friend's house. Aside from the street lamps, the night sky was pitch black. This occurred only a few streets down from city hall where a flying saucer was seen hovering above. As the boys were walking along Main Street near Orchard Street, a bright light emerged from the sky above them. Lighting up the surrounding area as if it were daytime. Instantly one of the boys took off at a full sprint, running away from the scene. The others didn't move, looking up, mystified.

A few seconds later a car approached and the boys tried to stop the car to show the driver the strange light above. The car wouldn't stop, driving off. They then tried flagging down the next vehicle which turned out to be a Leominster Police cruiser. The officer, stopped, exited his vehicle and looked up into the night sky. All he could see was the bright light engulfing him and the boys.

The police officer reached for his radio and was about to call into dispatch, but had no idea what to tell them. What were they looking at? The boys then suddenly found themselves back at one of their houses. They were on the front lawn and the boy who took off running was now with them again. They didn't know how they suddenly ended up at the house. We don't know what happened with the police officer involved or his identity.

The others asked the boy who ran away from the light, why he did it. He proclaimed that he felt that they were coming for him, so he decided to run. Sounds like he has had some previous experiences. It is also reminiscent of a classic case of "missing time" and alien abduction. Missing time is often reported with UFO abductees when it seems a few minutes have passed but in actuality, hours have gone by, like the Betty and Barney Hill case in New Hampshire. Sometimes it can be even days like with the Travis Walton abductee case in Arizona.

While researching for this book, I uncovered another encounter that occurred in Leominster and sounds exactly like a certain area that we have experienced a lot of strange phenomena, Leominster State Forest. It was found on *About.com* and entitled *UFO Encounter in Massachusetts* and written by Christina D.:

> *In April of 1999, my best friend, five guys that we had been hanging out with at the time, and I had gone to a wooded area in Leominster, Massachusetts. I cannot remember exactly where in Leominster these woods were located, but I do remember that it was off of a very quiet back road.*

*It was sometime after midnight. We got out of the car and approached a closed gate. We walked around the gate and walked along a path that was wide enough for a car or truck to travel and was still covered by thick ice, even though the temperatures had started to warm up recently. Along the left side of the path were trees and along the right side of the path was water. We walked for approximately a half mile before we started to travel on another path through the trees that followed a small creek. I'm not sure how long we traveled on this path. It was probably only 15 minutes at the most.*

*We came to a small clearing where there were still trees mostly surrounding us, but they were further apart, and there was a lot more room for us to walk around. We were surrounded by trees on three sides, but to the right was a lake or a pond. At the part that we were at it was only about 25 feet to get to land on the other side of the water where the trees were so thick that you could not see through them at all. To the left, the land ended and there the water went further out. I could not tell how far exactly, but at least a quarter mile. When we all got to this point we seemed to split up for some reason. My best friend and I walked to the edge of the trees to look at the water and four of the guys went in the direction opposite of us further into the woods while one of the guys traveled on along the path.*

*I'm not sure how long we were standing at the edge of the water; it seemed like forever, but in actuality, it was probably only about 10 minutes. Then, above the trees that were across the water from us, I saw a bright light moving toward us, which seemed to be hovering right over the trees. I started to feel very nervous and asked my friend what she thought it was and she said it was probably only a plane or a medical helicopter or something, but I knew that it was too close and it wasn't making any noise at all.*

*I called over to the guys that we were with to come over and take a look and they came running over saying, "Look, it is coming. I told you this is where we saw it!" Needless to say, I started freaking out. If I would have known that they were taking us for a long trek through the woods to see if we could see a UFO, I would NOT have gone!*

*Three of the guy's had been in these woods before when they had seen the same thing and they had decided to see if they could show it to the other two guys. My best friend and I just happened to be along for the ride because they needed her to bring them there because she was the only person with a car. My whole body was extremely tense by then and I just wanted to leave. This thing was starting to travel across the water now to our side of the trees, and just seeing it in the air and the reflection on the water freaked me out more and more.*

*My best friend seemed to shut down in shock or something and was not comprehending anything at this point. I was trying to tell her that I needed to get out of there right NOW! She didn't understand why at this point; it seemed like she was mentally blocking this whole experience out so she didn't understand my urgency to leave.*

*I told the guys to get us out of the woods right away, and they said no and that they weren't going anywhere at the moment. I didn't feel like fighting with them I just wanted to leave, so I asked them how to get back and they would not tell us. I gave up asking and was determined to find the way out, so I started to pull my friend by her arm to try and find the creek that we had followed to get to this point. I looked up again and it was right over our heads.*

*It was not really big like I would have expected it to be. It was round like a basketball and seemed only about five feet in diameter. It was emitting red and blue lights but they didn't seem to be coming from any one spot that I could see on the object, and it also did not seem to have any sort of pattern to the way the lights were emitted. The only way that I can really describe the lights in words is to say that it seems almost like they were tie-dyed and constantly changing.*

*I wanted to run through the woods to get out, but my friend wasn't hurrying up and this path was still icy in spots, although not nearly as bad as the main path. As we walked, this thing just kept following us right above our heads the whole time. I thought I was going to die. Every single hair on my body seemed to be standing on end and my heart was racing so fast I thought I was going to have a heart attack at 18 years old. I wanted to just stop and curl up in a ball, but I knew that I could not stop walking. After walking for what seemed like forever, I saw the main path up a little ice covered hill through the trees. I started pulling my friend along even more urgently.*

*She made it up the path before me with no problem, but when I went to go up it, I kept on sliding back down. I started crying frantically and begging God to help me make it up that hill. I had to get down on my hands and knees and crawl up that hill, but I finally made it. We started walking along the main path as quickly as possible, but my friend kept on falling flat on her back and hitting her head on the icy ground.*

*It amazed me that she never seemed to see this thing that was following right over our heads. Whenever she fell, I would stop to help her up and the object would just stop right over us. When we started moving again, so did it. It took us at least twice as long to walk that path back to the car then it had to walk from it. It was like the faster we walked, the longer it took.*

*Finally, I could see the gate, which meant the end of the path. I thought that I was never going to see it. The UFO followed us all the way up to the gate where it stopped. We got into the car and locked all the doors and I just watched it hover there the whole time we sat there. I tried to get her to leave the guys there and just drive us away, but she didn't seem to realize what was going on. The thing didn't go away until the guys got back to that point about an hour and 15 minutes after we did. When they got to the gate, it just disappeared.*

*The guys got into the car and we left. They kept on saying how awesome it had been that they had seen THEM in the woods. I didn't ask what THEY were. I just wanted to get as far away from there as possible. To this day, my best friend does not remember anything that happened that night in the woods. I will never forget it, though, and I will never go back into those woods ever again* (16)

The area of Leominster has been plagued with Bigfoot, UFOs and weird balls of light typically referred to as orbs. I began to ponder why Leominster was so special that the residents and local cities and surrounding towns have been experiencing these phenomena for decades. I felt strongly that these were somehow interconnected.

I grew up on Spruce Street in French Hill in Leominster up until I was about ten years old. My family then bought a house on Union Street, directly across from Fall Brook Farm. The farm consisted of an apple orchard and a small pond. If I wasn't riding my bike, I was across the street at the pond.

I would spend most of my summer days catching fish, frogs or snakes. It was a great neighborhood. I used to be able to take my bike and ride for miles into Sterling or Clinton and be gone all day long. My parents never worried. It was a different time back then compared to how it is now.

I also lived about five houses down from Fall Brook School. I would venture into Monsterland and the surrounding woods for hours on end. I recently found out that one of our neighbors' houses on Union Street, facing the school, was watching UFOs on a nightly basis. He confided in a friend of mine's father with his "secret". He hadn't told a soul for fear of being ridiculed. He would awake in the middle of the night, usually around 3:00 AM. He would make his way to the front porch and with Monsterland in view, he would then sit and wait.

In the distance, above what is known as Monsterland, are these enormous power lines. He would watch as UFOs would come to these power lines and charge up for several minutes, glowing incessantly, and then zoom off into the darkness. He said that this would happen almost every night! And that there were a multitude of ships that would be seen in any given time if you watched long enough.

With the city's long history of UFOs, I believe his story. I remembered an incredibly vivid dream that I once had when I was living on Union Street. I have never forgotten the dream and I can still picture the scene in my mind. I often wonder if this was truly a dream or if this really happened to me.

In my "dream", I awoke from a deep sleep and then headed downstairs to the kitchen. I approached the kitchen door and opened it. Through the storm glass door, I looked down the street to my next door neighbor's house and watched a UFO slowly moving above Union Street. It was the classic saucer-type, colorful lights were emanating from the craft. It stopped, hovering directly above my neighbor's house.

I watched as my neighbor walked out his front door walking to the end of his driveway and stopped directly underneath the UFO. He looked as if he was in a zombie-like state, standing there, waiting to be picked up. It was as if he had done this several times before. The UFO then shot a bright white beam of light which engulfed him. Instantly, he was sucked up into the light.

Then the light shut off. The UFO then slowly moved in the direction of my house and that's all I remember. I don't remember shutting the door. I don't remember opening the door and walking out. I woke up. The dream still gives me the chills. People typically don't remember dreams so vividly from over thirty years ago. I began to question whether it was a bad dream or a memory that I was supposed to forget.

When I was reading the book "*Incident at Exeter*", the author John Fuller described several locations where UFO sightings were taking place. They were seen at or near various hills. I couldn't help notice the similarities of the different hills and the ones that we have in Leominster. I wondered, could there be something under these domes of earth that attract the UFOs?

What I found intriguing was the fact that author John Fuller remarked that at least half a dozen people he had spoken with regarding their personal UFO sightings, mentioned that these UFOs were being seen over and near electrical power lines. UFOs were repeatedly witnessed over these high tension wires which cut across the country delivering power to the surrounding communities. Fuller stated that he would plan to follow up with this trend because several of the locations most popular for the flurries of reports were at the base of these power transmission lines.

Fuller states the obvious that if there were any truth at all to the theory that UFOs were operating on electromagnetic principles, there could be an affinity of the objects for the power lines, which could then possibly set up an electromagnetic field around them. (17)

On another note, Zoologist and UFO researcher, Ivan T. Sanderson, noticed that over fifty percent of all so-called "sightings" of UFOs have occurred over, coming from, going away over, or plunging into or coming out of the water. (18)

Taking that even further, in his book *Ultraterrestrial Contact* by Philip Imbrogno, the author reviewed one hundred and twenty-four cases of UFO sightings at a very low altitude (at water level, less than fifty feet). These UFOs were all triangle in shape. In all of these cases, the objects chose artificial lakes and reservoirs. There were no low-altitude sightings over natural lakes.

In every artificial lake and reservoir investigated, he found a compass deviation between .32 and .8 degrees. Indicating the presence of a magnetic anomaly. The natural lakes showed only a maximum of .10 degrees deviation. So the objects were more attracted to the man-made bodies of water and their magnetic anomalies rather than the naturally occurring lakes. Imbrogno believes that the reason that the UFOs are attracted to these bodies of water is due to the geological features below.

Most of the area has iron ore in its substrate composition, high-grade magnetite. The natural lakes were formed during the last Ice Age when glaciers carved out the rock below and made the basins that later filled with water from the melting ice sheets. However, the glaciers didn't expose all the iron ore. There was a thick layer of granite which remained on top. The use of heavy machinery and blasting to create the artificial lakes caused the depth to be much deeper than the natural lakes. This exposed more of the iron ore, which in turn creates a stronger magnetic anomaly within these bodies of water. (19)

The UFOs have been reported to charge up over these bodies of water like they have been seen to do with power lines. Imbrogno is also confident that they need to do this for a very important reason. He states that the craft could not necessarily be of an extraterrestrial origin, but of an interdimensional one, a parallel universe perhaps.

Due to the magnetic anomalies within these manmade bodies of water, there could be some sort of bend in space time allowing the craft to enter and leave our universe. The UFOs could very well be using the power lines or the magnetic anomalies from the artificial lakes to "charge up" which could allow them the ability to return to where they came from. Possibly another dimension.

# EARLY UFOS IN MASSACHUSETTS

In early September of 2014, I was home in the backyard with the kids on a beautiful weekend day. The sky was so blue and clear you could see for miles. There wasn't a cloud in the sky. We were cleaning up the yard, picking up toys that were strewed all across the lawn, when all of a sudden my daughter Lena looked up at the sky and said "Whoa! What's that?!" We all looked up directly above us and saw this somewhat boomerang shaped craft at an altitude of what seemed higher than what a normal airplane would fly. It was completely silent.

At first, when I looked up, it resembled a flock of geese flying together in formation. My mind accepted this as fact, but then after a few seconds of focusing on what I was looking at, that thought slipped out of my mind. As I started to follow the movement, these cross-shaped pieces, like the addition sign +, (which I assumed were geese flying in a V-formation) were not flapping their wings. They were also not flying in and out of formation as a normal flock of birds. There was no sound at all. They were black shapes, which I thought could be drones. As I looked closer, all of these pieces didn't seem to be flying in formation but were actually all part of one craft!

It was as if this vehicle, was cloaking or invisible and those spots we were seeing were where the lights would be. This was very similar to light placement patterns on other UFOs that have been videotaped around the world.

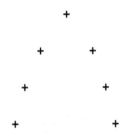

What sent shivers down my spine was when I looked where this thing was coming from, two military looking planes, not jets, but almost like smaller versions of C-130's were following it. They were both flying close together in formation following this craft or whatever we were looking at, but from a safe distance behind. One plane in front of the other.

My other daughter, Aysia exclaimed that this was exactly what her cheerleading team had all watched over the Pop Warner field the previous week. But it wasn't flying...it was hovering! I kept on looking at the craft. I didn't want to look away. I have read so many stories where people have witnessed something incredible and then they look away for a split second and what they are watching suddenly disappears.

"Aysia, you saw that same craft over the field, but it wasn't flying? It was hovering in the sky?! Same altitude?!" I asked. I finally lost sight of the planes that were following and looked down at Aysia, her head bobbing in confirmation that this is what she witnessed. She was watching them as well. "No doubt about it", she said.

My daughter is pretty serious when it comes to stuff like this. This confirmed to me that this wasn't a bunch of drones hovering in the sky together, but possibly we witnessed one craft. A week before the cheerleading coach had noticed that the girls were looking at a "flock of geese". She told the girls to pay attention and get back to practice. A few moments later, my daughter looked back in the direction of where this craft was hovering. It was now gone.

I wondered if this was a real UFO and if my daughter did see the same one...twice. The probability was high that it was a flock of drones, but I had my doubts it was a secret military aircraft. If it was something "Top Secret", you wouldn't want to fly it over a heavily populated area during the middle of the day.

When I look at the history of UFOs in Massachusetts and when they made their first appearance, it became quickly apparent that these crafts were not "Classified Projects" or secret aircraft that our Government was working on. Some of these are truly unidentified and quite possibly from somewhere else. People have seen dirigibles, flying saucers, triangles and also boomerang shaped craft. They have been seen in the skies for a long time. A long time before flight.

In *New England's Visitors from Outer Space*, which was published in 1970 and written by Robert Ellis Cahill, the author tells the tale of several strange bright disc-shaped objects flying in the sky way before we would even attempt the feat. These UFOs could be the first ever seen and recorded above the Atlantic Ocean, not too far from the shores of Massachusetts. These *disc-shaped* objects darted back and forth in "sudden and passing gleams". A sailor, Pedro Gutierrez, called the skipper on deck from his cabin to show him the spectacle in the sky. The year was 1492 and Christopher Columbus thought that they were interesting, but he had other things on his mind. He was to discover America three hours later that day on October 12th. (20)

There were unexplained lights in the sky in 1639 over the Charles River in Boston. From the Back Bay to Charlestown, lights sped back and forth across the Charles. This is an estimated distance of two miles. What is peculiar is that this also sounds like one of the first cases of "missing time".

It was significant enough of an event that even then Governor of Massachusetts, John Winthrop wrote about it in his own journal:

*"In this year one James Everell, a sober, discreet man, and two others saw a great light in the night at Muddy River. When it stood still, it flamed up, and was about three yards square; when it ran, it was contracted into the figure of a swine: it ran as swift as an arrow towards Charlton [Charlestown], and so up and down [for] about two or three hours. They had come down in their lighter about a mile, and, when it was over, they found themselves carried quite back against the tide to the place they came from. Other credible persons saw the same light, after, about the same place."* (21)

In 1765, something described as a black cloud-like object made its first appearance above Massachusetts over a decade before the country's Independence Day. It was called the "Flying Giant". Interestingly, it showed up on the same day that New Englanders were protesting the Stamp Act that was passed six months earlier by British Parliament. They were parading through the streets of Boston for the first time in protest of this act, which forced them to pay taxes for every legal transaction that occurred within the colonies. Many of the day believed that the Flying Giant appearing was God's way of protesting the

Stamp Act.

It appeared in the skies above Boston on August 14th, 1765 and was described by the *Boston Gazette and Country Journal*:

*"Dry weather – a black cloud-like object approximately the shape of a human body hovered over Boston and remained until Sunset, and thousands saw it. At 7:00 PM, the cloud landed, but quickly rose again and moved South only about twenty feet off the ground – down the main street, blowing a little vapor smoke intermixed with a few rapid sparks of electric fire, till it came before the Province House. Here, it flopped a few minutes, swelled, looked excessively black and fierce and suddenly discharged itself of three tremendous peals of thunder, which shook the lofty fabric and all the little houses, and hollow hearts did hear it. It shook and tore away a newly erected building said to be for a Stamp Office. Then it went up to Fort Hill where it shattered windows and delicate china in the home of the Governor and tore away his garden fence and coach-house door. It then ascended the mount at the same distance from the earth, where it stopped for a few minutes and it began to roar, and blow, and bellow, and thunder, and to vent smoke and fire, and raged like Aetna in ten thousand flames. It continued to behave in this ferocious manner until about 11:00 PM when it suddenly vanished and all was quiet once more."* (22)

What stands out to me is that this "cloud" shaped like a human body and emitting "thunder and smoke and fire" resembles many descriptions of UFOs. This human-shaped cloud also seems to have made a reappearance.

During the Revolutionary War, The Flying Giant returned, first seen in New Hampshire, then it headed south towards

Newburyport and then hung around Byfield, Massachusetts before departing. It was black and in the shape of a giant person about twenty feet high and this time it didn't cause any damage but seemed to cause quite a stir.

The cloud was described by a Deacon by the name of Daniel Chute of Byfield, who wrote in his journal that this black mass was "walking through the air", about two or three feet off the ground, going through fences and walls. The form curiously screamed "Hoo-Hoo" as it passed which caused several women to faint. This shape was thought by the colonists to be the devil and it made an appearance due to Pastor Parson of the Parish having slaves.

Flying saucers seem to have visited Massachusetts long before one was reported to have crashed in Roswell, New Mexico. And way before man had achieved flight. In the fall of 1833, during two days, on November 12th and 13th, there was an aerial display of lights in the sky. There were hundreds of thousands of objects that were shaped like jellyfish, others like "square tables", fireballs and shooting stars that appeared over Boston.

There was an estimated 300,000 of these objects that seemed to be concentrated above the city! They didn't just make their appearance at night. There were large fireballs seen during the daytime as well over the course of these two days. There were shooting stars with long tails and there were also objects described as, "stationary luminous bodies" as well as "dish-shaped objects" that were seen darting in and out of this meteor shower.

William Denton, a man from Massachusetts, declared a few years later after these events that he, his wife and children had visited the planets, Mars and Venus. He explained that they were taken in a flying saucer by aliens that looked just like humans. The craft was made out of what was described by Denton as being similar to aluminum, which wouldn't be made for another fifty years, until 1886. He reportedly published a tour guide of the planets. (23)

A few nights before Orson Welles' adaption of War of the Worlds that ran on the radio on Halloween, which would create utter panic as Americans thought that there was a real alien invasion, a UFO made an appearance in Somerville, Massachusetts.

It was 1938, and Malcolm Perry witnessed a cigar-shaped object steadily moving slowly against the wind in the night sky above him. He was walking home from a date on the streets of the city of Somerville when all of a sudden he looked up and noticed a UFO. There were no propellers and the object was pointed at both ends and silvery in color.

There were four rectangular portholes visible with orange light emanating from the inside of the craft. Malcolm could see a person in the craft, as it was only a few yards above him at this point, looking down at him.

Malcolm looked around and noticed that there were no other witnesses to what he was seeing. There was no one else in sight. When he looked back up at the craft, there were now several silhouettes visible through the portholes. They were looking down at him, taking turns! The sighting lasted about a minute before the craft then disappeared behind some low cloud cover. A similar cigar-shaped craft made an appearance over the Christmas holiday in Worcester, twenty-nine years later in 1909.

# 4

# THE MYSTERY AIRSHIP OF 1909

I had asked my mother if she had seen any UFOs while she was growing up near Worcester in the neighboring town of Leicester. To my utter shock, she replied that she had indeed seen one. She recalled that this occurred during the summertime when she was a child, maybe about ten years old. They lived next to a reservoir that they would sneak onto and fish. This was during the 1950's.

What's intriguing to note is that during this time period, Leicester was the location of something very strange that has happened numerous times across the globe during our recorded history. On September 7th, 1953, a downpour of frogs and toads "of all descriptions" began falling from the sky over Leicester, Massachusetts. The streets seemed to be alive with them and children gathered them into buckets using their hands, making a game of the astounding event. Officials attempted to explain the sudden appearance of thousands of the creatures by saying that they had escaped from a nearby, overflowing pond - however, this explanation did not provide a logical reason as to why so many of them were found on the roofs of houses and in the rain gutters! (24)

After one of these long summer days spent at the reservoir fishing and catching frogs, my mother and the neighborhood kids started to head home. It started to get close to dusk and the sunlight was quickly disappearing. Emerging from the woods, she crossed the road. She walked onto her driveway she looked up and saw an enormous black triangle-shaped craft hovering in the sky above her neighbor's house! She said that it was so big that it stretched across the sky.

She felt sudden fear and bolted straight for the front door and barged inside her house. She doesn't remember much after that. She hasn't seen another since. This was a triangle shaped craft near Worcester in the 1950's. I couldn't believe it. I started to dig into the UFO sightings and was astonished to find that Worcester is indeed a part of UFO history, but before there was any real air traffic in the sky...1909.

During the years of 1896 and 1897, parts of the country, including Massachusetts, reported seeing "cigar-shaped" objects. There were sightings in April of 1897 across Michigan, South Dakota, Texas and Washington, but they weren't the traditional flying saucers. They were cigar shaped or large dark forms with lights attached. There were over 1,000 sightings during this time period and it inspired the writer H.G. Wells years later to pen the world famous story "War of the Worlds", which was serialized in the Boston Post. (25)

In the early 1900's, there were multiple reports from all over the world of "airships" and they were reported to the newspapers of the day. Something to note is that in 1910, there were only 36 licensed pilots, which outnumbered the amount of planes that were in the air. These airships seemed to have taken an interest in central Massachusetts. In Jeff Belanger's book *Weird Massachusetts*, Worcester seems to be the epicenter of these sightings!

*In July 1909, newspapers in New Zealand and Britain were already theorizing that the lights in the sky were flying machines peopled by creatures from another planet. By the end of that year, most newspaper reports seemed to assume that the epicenter of this activity was Worcester, Massachusetts.*

*The Worcester sightings began the Wednesday before Christmas, when crowds on the street saw a strange moving light, apparently the searchlight of a dirigible. The following night, similar lights appeared in Marlborough, South Framingham, Natick, Ashland, Grafton, North Grafton, Upton, Hopedale, and Northborough. And in Fitchburg, according to the Christmas Eve issue of the Fitchburg Sentinel, "Over the peak of Rollstone Hill, a wonderfully bright light glowed, and hundreds watched it with wonder, not unmixed with awe."*

*The spate of sightings reached a fever pitch on December 23 in Boston's North Station, when the Evening Limited rolled northward on the Boston and Maine Railroad. As it approached Ayer, a messenger on board looked out of the window to see a cigar-shaped object descend from on high and hover above the train. The Fitchburg Sentinel takes up the story:*

*He says the powerful light of the ship played upon the cars of the train, and it followed along until this city was reached. Then it temporarily disappeared and was not picked up again until the train got up the line and for some time the light played over and around the cars. (26)*

You will note later on how the lights in the sky seem to be "playing" with one another in future UFO cases. This shows that there was some sort of intelligent control behind them and they seemed to have had the ability to maneuver beyond what we were capable of doing at that point in time. In what some consider to be one of the first stories of a UFO contactee in Massachusetts, a Worcester man claimed to have invented a flying craft.

During the month of December in 1909, there were "Airship" sightings continuing to pop up all over the country. But there was a figure, an inventor who claimed to be the one flying this airship around. He became the focus of the newspaper stories. He came forward as soon as the sightings of the mystery airplane broke out in the newspapers. And the national press took him seriously.

What's interesting is that he had this press conference in Worcester, before the UFO flap would even start showing up across New England. His name was Wallace E. Tillinghast and he was the Vice President of the Sure Seal Manufacturing Company in Worcester, Massachusetts. He held several patents.

Journalist and author John Keel did extensive research on this case. In his book *Operation Trojan Horse*, Keel talks about how Tillinghast claimed that he had invented, built and tested an airplane which was "capable of carrying three passengers with a weight limit of 200 pounds each, a distance of at least 300 miles without a stop to replenish the supply of gasoline, and if necessary at a rate of 120 miles per hour."

He described his invention as being a monoplane weighing 1,550 pounds, with a wingspread of 72 feet and an engine of 120 horsepower. It could take off in a small area of about 75 feet, stating he could travel at the amazing speed of 120 miles an hour, 2 miles a minute. Scientists believed at the time that a human being couldn't go faster than 60 miles an hour and live to tell about it. The inventor's monoplane was larger than anything that could be successfully flown at the time. (27)

Mr. Tillinghast claimed to have flown to New York City and around the Statue of Liberty back to Boston and back to NYC and...back on September 8th, 1909...all without landing. There was another incident during one of its aerial voyages where the motor stopped running and as it just sailed for forty-six minutes aloft, two mechanics repaired it in midair and got the motor going again. It sounds too good to be true. Tillinghast then claimed he had made, "Over 100 successful trips, eighteen of which have been in his perfected machine. His latest airplane is so perfect and adjusted so correctly that upon being taken from the shop it immediately made uninterrupted trips covering fifty-six miles." (28)

According to John Keel, one of the first published sightings, perhaps the very first of the UFO flap, appeared in the New York and Long Island newspapers. A Long Island lifeguard was among those that claimed to hear an airplane engine passing directly overhead while on night patrol. He saw nothing in the dark sky yet told reporters of the New York press his story the same day that the mystery inventor held a press conference in Worcester and revealed his marvelous discovery to the world, only the craft was never revealed.

Someone was flying this craft or a similar one while our illustrious inventor was doing his press conference. I questioned if Tillinghast had indeed invented the craft and if he was its pilot, why didn't he reveal the craft at the press conference? If I were Tillinghast, I would want to make a big splash at the press conference by taking off in midair with my mystery airship for all to see.

There was a sighting of an unusual light in the sky, a searchlight similar to that of an automobile and that it fluttered up and down like a bird at the same time...in Arkansas. Was Tillinghast outright lying as being the source of the Airship? For the next few days, the skies were silent across the country.

On Monday, December 20th the light show began right after midnight in Arkansas as a strong light seemed to probe across the sky...then something visited Boston Harbor at 1:00 AM. A bright light passed over the city. It was speculated that it was an Airship by the New York Tribune on December 21st, 1909 based on the statement by Immigration Inspector Hoe who was at the Harbor. According to Keel, the real flap began the next night in Pawtucket, Rhode Island on December 21st. At about 1:15 AM "Two red lights proceeding southward...all were able to make out the outline of the flying machine against the background of the stars" (29)

At 5:20 PM on Wednesday, December 22nd, a brilliant light appeared over Marlborough. Its powerful "searchlight" sweeping the sky. Then it slowly proceeded to Worcester, sixteen miles away, where it hovered above the city for a few minutes and then disappeared for two hours. Finally, it returned and circled four times around the city of Worcester, "using a searchlight of tremendous power. Thousands of people thronged the streets to watch this mysterious visitor."

The newspaper reporters rushed to Tillinghast's home but he was nowhere to be found. His wife told them that her "husband knows his business. He will talk when the proper time comes."

The next night all of New England seemed to be watching the skies and looking for the strange lights. Due to the fact that the lights were flying against the wind, balloons were ruled out as possible culprits. The strange lights were seen that night flying over Boston Common. There were a lot of sightings of lights in Marlborough, as well as South Framingham, Natick, Ashland, Grafton, North Grafton, Upton, Hopedale, and Northborough. That playful nature I mentioned earlier was back. There was an object that appeared to contain a search light that "played from side to side" and passed over Willimantic, Connecticut.

There is a great summary of the night's events in *The Providence Journal*, Rhode Island from December 24, 1909:

*As on Wednesday night, the light was first reported passing over Marlborough about 6:45 PM the light which was at a height so great as to make the impossible view of its support, disappeared to the southwest in the direction of Westborough and Worcester. It was traced from North Grafton, not far from Worcester, through Grafton, North Grafton, Hopedale, and Milford, and then after being lost sight of reappeared in Natick about 7:30 PM, going in the direction of Boston. Observers are positive that it was a searchlight. At 7:45 PM, it was seen from Boston Common, by the testimony of several persons, among them men who were at a prominent clubhouse in Beacon Hill.*

*At Northborough and Ashland, early in the evening, the population turned out en masse to watch the light pass overhead. Observers at several points report that while the light was generally steady, occasionally it flashed, and once or twice it disappeared entirely. (30)*

A statement from Tillinghast to reporters that night as he was not in the sky and tracked down, Tillinghast stated:

*I was out of Worcester last night. Where I was is my own business. It may be that I flew over the city, but that is my own business, too. When I said recently that I had flown from Boston to New York and returned, I said nothing but what was true. I have an airship which will carry three or four persons and will make the speed I claimed for it – that is, about one hundred miles an hour.*

*When I get ready, I will speak fully and not until then.*
(31)

There were more lights over Rhode Island, Connecticut, and Massachusetts on December 24th and the "searchlight" was frequently described by the witnesses of these airship sightings. Reporters continued to hammer Tillinghast for answers, but he was elusive to the press. He got calls at his office and at home constantly and was being watched by mysterious men at his place of business and at home.

On December 30th, due to pressure from the local board of trade in Worcester, the inventor would finally reveal more details. The board was upset with the hoopla this machine had brought the city. They demanded that he show proof of his claim of this "machine". The inventor would speak, but Tillinghast now did it through a spokesman, William Hunt. Hunt stated that the "machine" would be displayed at the Boston Aero show that was planned for the week of February 16-23, 1910. (32)

The sightings stopped and the machine never surfaced. This machine, this enigma of the Worcester skies was only seen at night. Where was it hiding during the day? There was a mysterious shed at the estate of John G. Gough, six miles outside of the city, near West Boylston. There were rumors that the Airship was hidden there and the owner of the property was supposedly friends with Tillinghast, as was Paul B. Morgan.

The shed, which was discovered hidden deep in the woods, was about one hundred feet in length. The right size for an airship everyone assumed. The story of the shed was revealed when it hit a widely published dispatch. It was picked up that a reporter, following the rumors of the city which then lead him to the area of the shed, was arrested for trespassing on the property where this secret was supposed to be. Trying to sneak a peek I am sure and with the intention of getting a prized photo of the airship.

The UPI dispatch reveals:

> There were fourteen men that were in the employ of the Morgan Telephone Company of this city and were working on some secret occupation. Paul B. Morgan, head of the telephone company, is a close friend of Wallace E. Tillinghast, who is supposed to be the inventor of the mysterious flying machine...Morgan had been interested in aviation for several years, and two years ago he spent $15,000 trying to perfect a machine invented by a Swedish aviator...proved unsatisfactory and was abandoned...the secrecy maintained at the Gough estate and the careful manner in which the shed discovered today is being guarded lends new weight to the belief that a marvelous ship has been constructed. The correspondent was taken before the justice summarily today, and the swift manner in which he was prosecuted for trespassing is believed to have been employed as a warning to others who might attempt to invade the secrecy of the airship plant. (33)

A year prior to the airship sightings of 1896 and 1897, a mysterious person, dark complexioned, dark-eyed and slight in nature, approached a well-known attorney in San Francisco and showed him drawings of a mystery machine that he needed help getting patents for. Curiously, he fit the description of the

Airship occupants that were seen during 1897. He asked the attorney, George D. Collins to play the "inventor" to the press. It was reported that this mysterious figure approached others on the west coast as well. The airship never materialized. History seems to be have repeated itself. Here's John A. Keel's theory on this mystery of Worcester, Massachusetts:

*Sometime in the fall of 1909, Mr. Wallace E. Tillinghast, one of the most prominent and reputable members of his community with a track record as an inventor, was approached by a man or a group of men who offered to take him for a ride in a marvelous new "secret" aircraft. Mr. Tillinghast was a man of science, and he was far too curious to reject such an opportunity. He went to an isolated field and climbed aboard the machine he found there. His hosts kept their promise and flew him around the countryside, perhaps even to Boston and back.*

*When they landed again, the pilots of the machine offered a proposition to Mr. Tillinghast. They struck a bargain (which they had no intentions of keeping), and perhaps they offered him a large interest in the profits from their flying machine, provided he did exactly as they ordered during the next few months. They explained that they needed a responsible, respectable man to front for them while they ironed out the bugs out of their invention. They appealed to his ego, saying that they were interested only in giving their airship to the world, and they didn't care if he took full credit for it. After the machine was fully tested, they promised, they would turn it over to him, and he could make all the arrangements for manufacturing more of them. He could also claim full credit for inventing it. They, the real inventors, would happily remain behind the scenes.*

*Mr. Tillinghast then accepted the proposition, visions of glory dancing in his brain. The machine had been proven to him. He was convinced of the reality of the trip he had taken. When reports of mystery airplanes started to filter into the press in early December, his mysterious friends called upon him and told him that it was time to disclose the existence of the invention. Tillinghast dutifully appeared before the reporters, revealed that he had already made a number of flights and that the invention would be fully unveiled at an appropriate time in the near future.*

*We can only guess at the contents of the shed on the Gough estate. Perhaps it was completely unrelated to the whole business. Or perhaps it housed special communications equipment supplied by the Morgan Telephone Company for the real "airship inventors." Mr. Morgan also had a known interest in aviation. He might have also been approached by "them" and was involved in the same deal as Tillinghast.*

*Whatever the case, thousands of people throughout New England observed UFO-type phenomena that Christmas week, and most believed that they were watching the wonderful invention of a local man. The objects flew orderly patterns over specific geographic points and performed maneuvers, which automatically ruled out conventional natural explanations. Morgan and Tillinghast were never given the promised model to back up their earlier claims. Like so many of the modern UFO contactees, they were used. (34)*

# 5

# HERE COME THE SAUCERS

The first time that I recall seeing a UFO was when I was in Canada. My father is originally from New Brunswick. I was nine years old at the time. The entire immediate family on my father's side each piled up their respective families and we headed north for the twelve-hour trek. We ended up staying in some family-owned cabins by the ocean.

There were large rocks exposed next to the shore that we were able to walk on. There was one particular rock that was big and flat enough for myself and two of my cousins to lay flat on our backs and view the pristine night sky. We were close in age and our parents let us stay up longer than normal since this was the first night of our vacation.

There was very little light pollution which allowed us the

ability to see deep into the night sky. I remember seeing so many stars it was almost as if we were looking at a completely different sky. We lost track of time as we were out there talking for hours about life and what we wanted to be when we grew up. It started to get really late, close to midnight. The conversation got pretty heavy for our ages. The topic of God came up and if there was any life on other planets was being discussed at the time. I asked the question if they believe we were the only ones in the universe. "Are we alone?"

Right when I asked that question I saw something. It looked like a star, white, slowly moving across the sky. I caught the movement when I had fixated on one point in the sky for several minutes. My eyesight had in time, adequately adjusted to view the evening stars with more detail. The "star" moved from the left of my vision and then to my right. I abruptly shouted "UFO! Right there! Can you see it?!" My cousin, who is now a Doctor, quickly surmised, deflated me instantly and said that what we were looking at was simply a satellite. I continued to watch it and reluctantly accepted this as fact. She was the smart one in the family. I took her word for it.

But then a minute or so later, we saw another star-like object going in a totally different direction. "If that's a satellite like the other one, then wouldn't they be following the same orbital path?" I asked. We saw yet another one going in the opposite direction. Another still another going from North to South. We started to count them. I believe we counted to eleven when we realized that the sky was alive. "Where are they coming from?" I asked. "Where are they going? Some of those may be satellites but others look like someone is behind the wheel!"

They changed directions, not abruptly, but enough that they didn't look like they were following some designated trajectory. We saw shooting stars. We saw several. But we saw these things moving slow and at some times, moving at an amazing clip of speed, but still visible, going in all directions. Their altitude had to be beyond earth's atmosphere. They were so far up that they matched the size of the majority of the distant stars. I wondered how big they really were. This memory has always stayed with me. The timing of seeing those "lights in the sky" coincided with the content of our conversation. It was like someone was answering my question about other life in the universe. From that moment on, I was a believer.

I became obsessed with finding more stories or cases of UFO sightings around my hometown and in Massachusetts. I continued to dig into the UFO history in Massachusetts. I searched for articles, books and started to review microfilm in Leominster Library to see if I could find any reports or sightings that might have made the local newspapers.

I wondered, just like with Bigfoot sightings, how many UFO sightings had occurred but were never reported to anyone, let alone the local police or newspaper. There were some significant sightings and cases within the state of Massachusetts from the past that are worth mentioning.

From the years 1947 (the year of the Roswell Crash and when the term "flying saucer" was coined) to 1969, there were over 4,429 UFO reports from New England, 1,910 of those are from Massachusetts. A year before in 1946, hundreds of people in Boston at South Station and Faneuil Hall saw a UFO shaped like a disc. It zoomed down silently and then flew away.

In March of that year, five grey, aluminum looking saucer-shaped UFOs, flying in formation, made appearances across Massachusetts. A man named Frank Strange from Bernardston happened to snap a photo of three of them flying together, with two others hovering in the sky. (35)

In 1947, a few cities away in Gardner, a disc-shaped UFO, which accelerated with a burst of speed, was observed at 5:48 PM by Warren Baker Eames. Mr. Earnes, president of an interior design company, was also a Magna Cum Laude graduate of Harvard University. While driving west on Route 2, Earnes noticed a large bright object in the sky. The UFO seemed to be traveling in the same direction. It was round, disc-shaped, exactly like a silver dollar in shape, with a silver, aluminum color. A few seconds later, the edge of the UFO slightly dipped down and the craft took off at a high rate of speed. (36)

There was a UFO sighting at a prominent east coast Air Force base around 1952. It was submitted as a confidential report to NICAP board member, Rev. Albert Baller of the German Congressional Church in Clinton, MA. A letter was sent to Rev. Baller from an Air Force control tower operator, dated March 10, 1954.

*"At about 3:00 AM, on a clear moonlight night, a buddy of mine who was a radar operator on the same night shift called me rather excitedly on the intercom and asked me if I could see any object in the sky about fifteen miles southwest of the base. Using a pair of powerful binoculars, I carefully scanned the sky in that direction and assured him that I could see nothing. It was then that he told me why he was so concerned.*

*For several minutes he had tracked an object on his radar scope, then all of the sudden it had stopped at a range of fifteen miles from the base and remained stationary. Being an experienced radar operator, he knew that whatever it was, it was of good size, at least as big as any one of our larger transport planes. But what amazed him was the fact that it stopped and remained motionless on the scope. A full half-hour passed and still, the object remained in the same location on the radar screen. Remembering that I had an inbound C-124 Globemaster coming in from that direction, I thought that perhaps the pilot would see something out there that we couldn't see. I gave the pilot a couple of calls and finally raised him just south of _____ on his way in. I told him what we had on radar and asked him if he would mind swinging off his course slightly so that he could take a look for us.*

*I then turned him over to the radar operator who had picked up the inbound aircraft on radar and guided the pilot to a new heading that would bring him directly into this blip that was still stationary on the screen. The pilot slowed his aircraft and he and his copilot and engineer started looking about them. I could hear the radar man giving the pilot directions on a monitoring speaker in the tower.*

*The aircraft got onto a line on the radar screen that would intersect the blip that was unidentified; then as the minutes went by, the aircraft slowly approached the object on the scope. Both blips were equally light and distinct. Then, when it seemed as if the two would collide, at about a half-mile separation on the scope, the stationary object simply disappeared, vanished seconds before the big Globemaster reached its location.*

*None of the crew on the plane had seen anything at any time, although they were all observing closely at the time and were told how close they were getting all the way to the object. How anything could vanish so suddenly from a radar screen without even leaving a trace of what direction it went is really amazing.*

*When you bear in mind that a radar scanner usually has a sweep of better of fifty miles, that would mean that whatever the object was, it went from a dead standstill at fifteen miles and disappeared from the scope, covering over 35 miles in a split second. Remember also that this object was there for over a half-hour and did not disappear until seconds before the aircraft reached its position. Certainly, this couldn't be any electrical disturbance or other phenomena. Why then would it disappear precisely when it did?"(37)*

In 1952, in Greenfield, a congregational minister observed three very bright silver objects, apparently of spherical shape, flying in a perfect V formation. (38) On July 11th in 1952, two silvery cigar-shaped objects were seen flying above Boston. In Braintree of that same year, an F-94 pilot and others vectored in on a UFO by radar saw a blue-green light, locked onto radar only to have the UFO speed away unscathed. (39)

There's a famous photograph of several UFOs flying in formation above Salem, Massachusetts, the city of the infamous Salem Witch Trials. At 9:35 AM on July 16th, 1952, Shell Alpert, who was a United States Coast Guard Seaman, saw four bright lights flying in formation while he was stationed at the base in Salem. He was sitting in his photographic lab and noticed these strange lights through his window.

He called another guardsman to come over to look at the lights, but they faded out when the other guardsman came to look. When they brightened again, he quickly took a single photo of the lights which was sent to Project Blue Book (Case #1501).

Project Blue Book was the Air Force's study on the UFO phenomenon. It studied cases from 1952 until it was given a termination order in 1969 and closing its operations in 1970. The objective was to determine if UFOs were a threat to National Security and to scientifically analyze the UFO data that was gathered. Project Blue Book would eventually proclaim the photo to be "unexplained", but it wasn't until the third completed analysis that they accepted this conclusion. Something to note, many researchers and insiders believe that Project Blue Book, like the Condon Committee and their report which was sanctioned by the U.S. Air Force, was simply a public disinformation campaign aimed at reducing the fears of the American public regarding UFOs. The government had no idea who or what was flying around in our skies.

The first explanation was that the lights were caused by a double exposure "hoax" and the second was that the lights in the photograph were a reflection on the window from some nearby street lamps. The time of day when the photo was taken was 9:35 AM. This would certainly nix the "street lamp" theory. Especially during the summer when the sun rises extremely early. It is still today probably one of the most recognized and popular UFO photos.

The lights in the Salem photo look like the "foo fighters" that the American pilots encountered in the skies during World War II as they flew over the European and Pacific theaters of operation. The term "foo fighters" was used to describe any UFOs seen during this time period. It was thought that these balls were the enemy's secret weapons. The other side thought that these lights were ours! These same type of UFO/lights were captured on film as well as radar by the Washington National Airport when seven of these were seen flying in formation over the Capitol in Washington D.C in 1952. [40]

In what sounds like a Steven Spielberg movie, in June of 1953 there was the disappearance of a Radio Operator and an

F-94C Starfire interceptor of the Air National Guard. It is believed that the jet was dispatched to intercept a UFO that failed to respond to radar identification as it was flying over Otis Air Force base in Cape Cod, Massachusetts.

This real event was written about in *Need to Know* by Timothy Good. There was a retired Master Sergeant by the name of Clarence O. Dargie, who was present at Otis Air Force base at the time of the incident. He completed a written report of the event.

The official accident investigation report that was obtained by reporter Bob Pratt from Norton Air Force Base stated: "The plane was up at 8,000 feet, had been up there 20 minutes, caught fire, and they both bailed out and the plane and the man in the back seat simply disappeared into the sea. And they refused to release to me the testimony of the pilot...claiming it would impugn his reputation" (41)

The interceptor had classified electronic gear on board at the time, and one wonders if it may have been some type of early thermal imaging trying to capture the elusive "foo fighters" and UFOs of the day. The crew that occupied that ironically named Starfire Interceptor was Radio Operator Lt. (Robert) Barkhoff and Pilot Captain Suggs.

Clarence O. Dargie was interviewed by investigator Raymond E. Fowler and the following is extracted from a written report by Dargie which also included the pilot's testimony. According to Dargie, this disappearance "caused one of the most extensive and intensive searches I have ever seen...the Cape was literally combed, both on foot and from the air for three months without turning up a thing." (42)

As soon as the F-94C Starfire Interceptor took off to intercept the aforementioned UFO, at about 1,500 feet, the pilot stated that they "were over the Base Rifle range "when the engine quit functioning and the entire electrical system failed." (41)

The pilot yelled to Barkhoff, the Radio Operator, to eject. The Radio operator would then, by following protocol, jettison the canopy by the means of explosive bolts that he could activate. Once clear he would then eject himself from the craft by way of an explosive device under his own seat. The pilot would then follow suit. This is normal procedure for this particular type of aircraft, but the pilot didn't wait for the second explosion and ejected immediately after the canopy was released due to the close proximity of the ground. It was estimated that they were three seconds away from the impact. Master Sergeant Dargie continues:

> "The parachute opened and acted as an airbrake to slow the pilot down and stopped his forward motion just as his feet hit the ground. He landed in the backyard of a house near the base, and the first indication that the owner had that there was something amiss was when he heard Captain Suggs calling out to his R/O, 'Bob, where are you?'
>
> The R/O could not be found and the pilot had a difficult time convincing the owner that his aircraft had crashed because the man had been sitting near and open-screened window and had heard nothing. The crippled plane should have crashed near where Suggs landed but it wasn't there...the aircraft had a full fuel supply aboard and if it did not explode into flames on impact, it would have left a large fuel slick on the surface...this whole event took place in a well-populated area at the height of the tourist season. If it did crash in that area, it would have created a detonation heard for miles; yet, no

*explosion was heard...As I recall, the canopy was found on the rifle range, which would indicate that whatever happened took place in close proximity to the airfield proper.*

*What caused the complete and simultaneous failure of all engine and electrical systems? The pilot swears that, without warning, the cockpit lights, navigation lights, instruments, radio, and engine simply went dead...Some of the circumstances involved in this case were classified and I have had to frame my story around them. Jets of this nature were dispatched to intercept aerial objects that failed to respond to radar identification. It was on just this type of mission that this aircraft vanished."* (43)

June 1st, 1954, near Boston, a TWA pilot coming from Paris, along with the control tower operator saw a large white disc. (44) On October 8th, 1957, again near Boston, a Pan American Airways pilot saw a brilliant object flying at high speed during the middle of the day. (45)

There were other interesting sightings that occurred in Massachusetts and New Hampshire as well as in Maine. I was able to strip all the UFO sightings away that occurred in Massachusetts from the whole list of cases that were covered in the comprehensive *The UFO Evidence* and *The UFO Evidence Volume II* by Richard H. Hall.

One particular sighting and an important abduction case to mention due to the close proximity of Massachusetts was the first known UFO abduction case in America. The Betty and Barney Hill case occurred on September 19th, 1961 in the White Mountains of New Hampshire. It is known worldwide. The couple had a close encounter with an unidentified flying object as they were driving along Route 3 near Lincoln. They reported seeing a brightly-lit cigar-shaped object with portholes and people. They made a report to Project Blue Book the following day. Their encounter was a secret until it was leaked four years later in 1965 by the *Boston Traveler*, which is now *The Boston Herald*. The couple also experienced two hours of "missing time." Their story became the first widely reported UFO abduction case in the United States. (46)

There is actually a marker in front of Cabin 20 at the Indian Head Resort in Lincoln describing the UFO incident. Interestingly, the location of the encounter is across the street from the granite stone face called Indian Head on Route 3. It is also known as "Old Man of the Mountain" or the "Great Stone Face". It was made up of five granite cliff ledges on Cannon Mountain. The famous New Hampshire landmark collapsed in 2003.

On October 11th, 1964, in Brockton, Massachusetts, an engineer and others observed a dome-shaped object following jet fighters. The UFO shot straight up and out of sight. At about 4:00 PM, David Hanson, an engineer who was with Vincent Flaherty, an accountant as well as a third friend, were startled when they heard two sonic booms. They looked up and saw two jet fighters leaving contrails. Behind them was a whitish, dome-shaped object. When the object caught up with the jets, it descended slowly over the city of Brockton and settled off into a horizontal path. It finally accelerated straight up and out of sight in a matter of seconds! (47)

What are these objects and where do they come from? The bigger question is who is behind them? On November 9th and 10th in 1965, there was a massive power blackout in the Northeastern United States that put the entire Atlantic seaboard under total darkness. What isn't widely known is that there were some reports of UFOS which coincided with this event, resulting in some speculation that perhaps there is a quite possibly a relationship or connection with the two.

A prominent physicist, Dr. James McDonald from the University of Arizona explained to United States Congress that *"there are too many instances of sightings of UFOs hovering near power plants. Particularly during the November 9th blackout in the Northeast, when the Federal power commission had hundreds of reports of UFO sightings."* (48)

The Northeast Blackout of 1965, caused a significant disruption in the supply of electricity on Tuesday, November 9th, 1965. Parts of Ontario Canada, Connecticut, Massachusetts, New Hampshire, New Jersey, Rhode Island, Vermont and New York were affected. (49)

In the book entitled *Alien Agenda* by Jim Marrs, The Northeast Blackout was an event that had something to do with the UFOs that were seen near these power plants. There was no real explanation for what happened:

*"Over the night of November 9th and 10th, 1965, a massive power blackout spread from Southern Canada to Pennsylvania, affecting some thirty million people. Nearly one million people were left stranded in the New York subway system. It was an event never to be forgotten by those who experienced it. And intriguingly, there were many rumors at the time linking the Great Blackout to UFO activity. Some years later, an abductee named Betty Andreasson claimed aliens admitted to her they had caused the blackout.*

*Immediately after the blackout, Washington officials and most power grid experts agreed that the problem began near the Clay power substation south of the giant Niagara Falls generating stations. However, no one had an explanation for why the blackout occurred. Charles Pratt, chief of the Niagara-Mohawk generating plant, said, "We have no explanation. There were no severed transmission lines, defective generators or faulty circuit breakers."*

*A Consolidated Edison spokesman commented, "We are at a loss to explain it." Even the chairman of the Federal Power Commission, Joseph C. Swidler, said after a two-day investigation, "The Northeast Blackout may never be fully explained..."*

*Others thought they had an explanation. The Syracuse, New York, Herald-Journal reported UFOs were seen near the Clay substation at the time of the blackout. On November 14th, NBC newsman Frank McGee reported that a pilot had sighted a UFO near Niagara Falls power plant just before the blackout. Other media outlets picked up and circulated the UFO connection. Someone within the government must have been concerned that such speculation might lead to in-depth investigations that might crack the secrecy over UFOs."*

*But all UFO speculation ended on November 15th, when it was announced that one broken relay in a Canadian power plant had started the whole thing. Somehow the broken relay had been missed despite an intensive five-day investigation. The explanation seemed to lull both the media and, hence, the public. But serious questions remain.*

*"There was only one true explanation – an unpredictable, overwhelming E(lector) M(agnetic) Interference the safety devices were not built to handle." – General Donald E. Keyhoe*

*If Keyhoe and Andreasson were correct and the Great Blackout was caused by UFOs draining power, it didn't stop there. Through the end of November and into December 1965, there were large-scale blackouts in Minnesota, both East and West Texas, New Mexico, and Mexico.* (50)

Under hypnosis, Andreasson was asked if the aliens had any hand in the notorious power blackout of 1965. She indicated they had caused it for the purpose of revealing to man his true nature. "They have powers," she said. "They can control the wind and water and even lightning." She said the visitors explained that the blackouts were caused to show man his true nature, namely that "Man seeks to destroy himself (through) greed...everything has been provided for man. Simple things. He could be advanced so far, but greed gets in the way...other worlds are involved in man's world. Man is very arrogant and greedy and he thinks that all worlds revolve around him."

She claimed to have been given information that seventy different aliens races – some come from the very Earth" – have been working for the betterment of mankind on Earth "since the beginning of time." These races all work together except for one that is an "enemy." (51)

"Other worlds are involved in man's world?" Where are these worlds? What are these worlds? Planets? Other dimensions intersecting with our own? Betty proclaims that some of these aliens come from this very earth. So many have dismissed Betty's story due to the sheer fantasy and science-fiction elements it seems to possess. How could any of this be true? Why are so many people having these sightings? Massachusetts is just a small microcosm of the entire planet that seems to be having these interactions that go back to the beginning of time. One thing to remember, it only takes one of these encounters to be true to make the entire phenomena real.

# THE SKIES ARE ALIVE

The years 1965 and 1966 were soaking in UFOs. We have the Northeast Blackout in 1965 that some have speculated was caused by the UFOs themselves knocking out the power grid in Niagara Falls. Then in 1966, there was a UFO wave that hit Massachusetts.

There were many sightings of flying saucers as well as orange orbs that plagued the state. A Gallup Poll in 1966 reported a 90% public awareness regarding UFOs and nearly half of the adult population in the US believed that UFOs were real.

Not only were UFOs in the sky, there was also an incident where a USO, an Unidentified Submerged Object, was seen in the Atlantic Ocean by military pilots. NICAP, the National Investigations Committee on Aerial Phenomena, was a UFO research group that investigated UFO cases from the 1950's through the 1980's.

During the year of 1966, the month being unknown, an active Air Force jet pilot, with the rank of captain, who was a NICAP member, came to Donald E. Keyhoe's office and reported that *"a group of Service pilots had seen a large disc-shaped object rotating under the surface of the Atlantic Ocean. The sighting was at night, while the pilots were on a routine mission, and the UFO was clearly visible because of its brilliant blue-green glow."* (52)

So we have several Air Force pilots unable to identify a craft that is described as a classic flying saucer, but submerged under water, rotating, and glowing blue-green. Whose technology is this way back in 1966? People were seeing things in Massachusetts that they had never seen before and encounters that they couldn't quite explain. Some that I am sure were never shared. The fact that there were so many of them within Massachusetts during this time period, it sounds as if the Bay State was being invaded. The question remained, where were they all coming from?

On March 29th, 1966, in Haverhill and Merrimack, several people saw a pulsating luminous white object moving back and forth. Its color changed from white to red to green to blue and back to white. The UFO then circled, hovered and then sped away. (53)

On March 30th in Rehoboth, three separate groups of witnesses had a series of sightings over a period of nearly two hours in the evening. This included an object with amber body lights that passed over a car and hovered off the road ahead. As soon as the car approached closer, the craft took off at high speed. It flashed its red body lights and emitted a humming or whistling sound.

In eastern Massachusetts on April 18th through the 20th, there was a concentration of sightings that included several reports of an egg-shaped object with red lights on each end. (54)

One of the cases that tend to be used as a weapon for the pro-extraterrestrial argument is the Beverly, Massachusetts sighting which involved Nancy Modugno and nine witnesses including police officers. (55)

This case was so significant that it was sent to the Condon Committee, which was a group assigned to study UFOs for the U.S. Air Force. This case, as were most of the significant ones at the time in Massachusetts it seems, were investigated by Massachusetts native and former Raytheon employee Raymond E. Fowler. He investigated this case on behalf of NICAP. He was an investigator with MUFON (Mutual UFO Network) and CUFOS (Center for UFO Studies) as well.

The events of that evening began to unfold shortly after 9:00 PM on April 22nd, 1966. An eleven-year-old Nancy Modugno, noticed a bright light blinking through her window as she lay in her bed. What she saw, only forty feet away, was an object the size of a car. It was all lit up with lights flashing blue, green and red. Shaped like a football, the object made a ricocheting and whizzing sound as it moved at a low altitude, flying over the neighborhood near Beverly High School. Nancy continued to watch the craft through her window as it flew behind some trees. It apparently found a resting spot and landed in a large field behind the school.

Nancy was terrified and ran down the stairs and tried to tell her father about what she had just seen. Her father was adjusting the television set as she came down in a panic. It had mysteriously lost its picture.

Claire, Nancy's mother, was visiting two friends, Barbara Smith and Brenda Maria, who were all in an adjoining apartment, during the time of the event. Nancy's father told his daughter to get back to bed, but she would not move and was so upset about what she witnessed. Nancy's mother and her friends entered the apartment to order a pizza during this episode of Nancy going into absolute hysterics.

They tried to calm her down. Her mother and her friends could clearly see the lights in the field. In order to ease Nancy's fears, they would walk over to the source of the lights and prove to Nancy that it was just a plane that she was seeing.

The ladies walked down a hill to where the "plane" was last seen. The three women looked up and saw three brightly lit objects, oval-shaped flying around in the sky. They had a playful nature to them. They looked as if they were playing tag, stopping and circling each other. One was directly over the school while the other two were a further distance away.

To get a closer look at the objects, the women crossed the field. They then could discern that the flashing lights on the edge of the craft were changing colors from red to green and then to blue. Brenda then waved her arms at the object and the object immediately stopped circling. It seemed to notice Brenda's movements and the women's presence because it slowly moved across the field toward them. At this point, the women became horrified.

In Barbara's statement, she said, "It started to come towards us...I started to run. Brenda called, 'Look up! It's directly over us!' I looked up and saw a round object...like the bottom of a plate. It was solid, grayish white...I felt this thing was going to come down on top of me. It was like a giant mushroom."

Barbara and Claire then turned and ran up the hill. Brenda was left all alone in the field to fend for herself. The object was now only twenty feet above her head. Barbara continued with her statement, "The object appeared larger and larger as it came closer. The lights appeared to be all around and turning. The colors were very bright. When overhead, all I could see was a blurry atmosphere and brightly lit-up lights flashing slowly around... I thought it might crash on my head!" When Barbara and Claire yelled to her to follow them, she finally did and ran to her friends. One of the witnesses was so scared by what happened she wet her pants. I would have too.

The women, in order to alert the neighbors, ran back to the apartment complex to let them all know what had just transpired. The UFO slowly moved over Beverly High School. A neighbor was already watching the flying saucers in her yard. Another man had seen the UFOs and called the police who soon arrived at the scene.

The officers, Bossie and Mahan sarcastically asked the group where the plane was. When they all pointed to the UFO, which was then at a higher altitude, now looking like a star, the officers began to laugh. Then, all of a sudden, the UFO turned bright red and dropped to a position directly over the school.

At this point, the officers stopped laughing. They were scared too. One of the officers, Mahan, elaborated further on what he had seen, "I observed what seemed to be a large plate hovering over the school. It had three lights – red, green, and blue – but no noise...this object hovered...the lights were flashing..." The other police officer, Bossie, had this to say, "It hovered and then began gliding. Some of the people got on the ground and were real scared!"

The officers then jumped into the cruiser and headed towards the direction of the object. At this point, they could see very clearly that this was no airplane or a helicopter. The shape was like that of a half-dollar with three lights, which were red, green and blue. There were also indentations at the rear of the disc, which looked almost like back lights.

The disc made a couple of passes over the school as the officers got out of the car. The UFO then moved. It started to move away slowly, but eventually, it disappeared as it picked up speed and went behind some buildings. Although no one saw the other UFOs leave, they were now gone. They had disappeared. (56)

It seems time and time again that the UFOs just simply disappear and vanish. Where do they go? There was a flurry of sightings in eastern Massachusetts during the month of April. This was a month after many UFO sightings in Michigan were deemed to have been solved. These sightings were simply caused by "swamp gas" explained the experts of the day. There were eighteen UFO sightings that were logged in from April 11th to April 23rd. They were seen in Danvers as well as Attleboro. There were at least six reports on two consecutive nights, April 19th and April 20th.

What is always compelling is when there are UFO sightings that involve police officers. They are trained observers. Police officers are considered some of the best witnesses due to their training and their experience on the job. They are constantly talking with and interviewing witnesses for their statements, looking for the truth.

At midnight on April 18th, when the May's of Sharon, Massachusetts, arrived home, they saw an egg shaped craft hovering over an adjoining field next to their home. It was hovering about five hundred feet above the ground. Due to a large band of yellow light that wrapped around the craft, it gave the Mays' the impression that they were looking at a row of windows. The craft stayed in this position for about ten minutes and then lifted up on a slant and then accelerated away at a rapid rate of speed, disappearing from sight.

The following night, a group of people descended upon the May's property to get a view of the UFOs that were seen the night before. Around the same time as the previous night's sighting, at 11:45 PM, a group of lights was spotted in the east. The lights were blinking in the same manner as the night before. Mrs. May quickly called the police and they dispatched two officers. They were relieved due to a shift change and Officer Frederick Jones and Sergeant Bernard Coffey arrived at the scene. It would only be a matter of a few minutes before the light show would begin again. Sgt. Coffey's report tells the story:

*About 12:10 AM, Officer Jones and I watched these distant lights with the Mays. One of these objects was in a northwesterly direction, similar to a star, only brighter. It appeared to be rotating and changing colors from red to white to green. There were two other objects of the same description in a southwesterly direction.*

*While we were observing these distant lights, Mrs. May said 'here it comes,' or 'there it is,' and we all looked in an easterly direction. The object appeared to be a falling star at a great distance, only three times the size of a star, and brighter. Within a matter of two or three seconds, the object appeared over the tree line on the easterly side of the field in front of the Mays' house about 200-300 yards away from us and approximately 500 feet up.*

*When it was hovering over the tree line it appeared as a very bright, large mass of white light with a ball-like [round] appearance. It made no noise whatsoever and did not cast any light onto the tree line or ground below.*

*"The object stopped and hovered over the tree line for approximately two or three minutes. While it hovered a plane passed over in a northerly direction. When the plane moved off, the object started to move across the field in front of us in a southwesterly direction. As the object passed in front of us I viewed a red light in front and a red light to the rear that remained on (not flashing) and a wide section of white light extending from red light to red light and there appeared to be inside lights. I concentrated on trying to see inside of the object for any figures or movements but failed to detect any signs of life or figures. I feel as if I did see inside the object. The object disappeared as it went over the tree line in a southwesterly direction."* (57)

There were sightings in and around the city of Sharon, on the night of the 19th and 20th by various witnesses like Mr. David Klapp of Sharon and Ms. Peggy Kudla of Bellingham, just a few miles west. It seems to me that we were being visited by someone and for whatever reason, they had a very strong interest in Massachusetts. *(58)*

Not everything "out of this world" happens in the east or central parts of the state. The west gets its share as well and one particular case has broken ground in getting closer to admitting that UFOs are real.

For the first time in US history, a Massachusetts-based UFO encounter and abduction case was accepted into the Great Barrington's Historical Society as a real event. The Thomas Reed UFO abduction case has been formerly inducted into the city's historical records. The *Boston Globe* reported on the monumental event on February 23rd, 2015:

*SHEFFIELD – This is how the story goes: It is 1966, and 6-year-old Thomas Reed is in his bedroom on his family's horse farm in the Berkshires when the encounters begin. Strange lights. Strange figures in the hallway. Suddenly, he's in the woods near his home looking at a UFO. Then he and his younger brother, Matthew, are inside the craft. He's shown a projection of a willow tree. The following year, there is another incident at their home on Boardman Street in Sheffield. More strange lights. The sound of doors slamming. Then the boys are back inside the vessel. The next thing Thomas knows, he's in his driveway being scooped up by his mother, who has been searching frantically for the boys on horseback.*

*Two years later, the family is driving on Route 7 when they see strange lights in the sky. Their car stalls, and then Thomas and his brother and mother and grandmother find themselves in a giant room. He is brought to meet two strange, ant-like figures, then placed in some sort of cage. Next thing, he's back near the car...*

*"It means that we believe it is true," said Debbie Oppermann, the director of the society. "I know we're going to get a lot of backlash. We're going to get hammered," she said. "But we have given it an awful lot of thought, and, based on the evidence we've been given, we believe this is a significant and true event."...The Reed case already has its own display in the International UFO Museum and Research Center in Roswell, N.M.; now, it's about to get one in Great Barrington, about 2 miles from where the alleged encounters took place.*

*What most interests the historical society is the 1969 encounter, because dozens of people in the area reported seeing an unidentified flying object around that time, typically described as a disk-shaped craft performing acrobatic maneuvers in the sky. Many of those eyewitnesses called the local radio station, WSBS, which covered the sightings. (The radio station has provided documentation to the historical society, which interviewed one of those eyewitnesses. They have also examined a polygraph test taken by Thomas Reed.)* (59)

There was a US as well as an International wave of UFO sightings during the months of January and May in 1967. There was another UFO wave during the months of July and December for the US as well as abroad. On January 6th, 1967 in Harwich, a disc with lights on its underside was seen. It pulsated colored lights and reacted to the switching of the outside lights on and off. The UFO would blink in the same sequence as the outside lights. This was included in an Air Force report for the Condon Committee. (60)

On January 9th and 10th in 1978, there was a UFO case involving a humanoid entity. In 1980, an article was written by David M. Webb, who reported the following occurrence in South Middleton. There have been other humanoid sightings there as well in the years 1962 and 1977. There were at least seven separate encounters involving Tom Gould. Tom spent much of his day on January 10th chopping wood on his property. There was some snow on the ground. At about 2:30 PM in the afternoon, about ninety feet away, Tom spotted a white-suited figure standing on a path beside a tree. The figure was about four and a half feet tall and wore a square helmet that had two dark eye or eyeholes. The being wore gloves and only three digits were noted.

*Upon finishing the chopping, Tom got in his pickup and drove down the road a short way. He looked again at the being but it was gone. (The area is hilly with lots of trees and shrubs. It is easy to lose sight of a small object even nearby.) Then he noticed what looked like a huge boulder about 150 feet away down a slope in a partially wooded area.*

*He stopped the truck, got out and walked some distance around the area to look for the being and to get a better vantage point on the strange object. The object was sitting on the ground; "it was egg-shaped, wider at the front than...at the back. It's got little windows all over the sides of it...The window looked like a frog's eye — it had a hood-like over the window," said Tom. Later Nancy reported the windows as round and bubble-shaped; they seemed to protrude from the sides of the craft and were adjacent to one another.*

*The dark gray surface of the UFO was dull and rough, like the surface of a brick. No seams or protrusions were evident. Measurements in the area indicated that the UFO was about 40 feet long by 13.5 feet wide across its nearer or wider end, and possibly 10 feet high (an undetermined portion lay in the snow or depressing the ground surface). The being had been approximately 300 feet to the west of the UFO. I investigated the "landing area" on April 23rd, or 3.5 months later; at that time it was well overgrown with brush and small trees.*

*There was no evidence of a depression or environmental damage except for broken limbs on two trees. These two trees were the tallest in what would have been the UFO's path of vertical descent. I was the one who first noticed these broken limbs, and pointed them out to Tom. He stated*

75

*he was sure they were broken by the UFO because they had not been broken before the sighting, and the wood had appeared green and clean-cut the day after the sighting. I questioned him closely on this point. He admitted that he could not be sure he had been in the area of the "landing" within several days to a week before January 10th.*

*Tom was afraid to approach close to the UFO and eventually returned home. He is uncertain when he told the family about his experience, but remembers that upon doing so they laughed and thought it was a joke. There is a discrepancy about whether the next sighting was the same day or the next day...*

*On the following day (probably January 12th), he observed a UFO about 100 feet in the air over a rise at an azimuth of 15°. Its bearing was approximately the same from the house as the location where the landed object had been but apparently closer to the house. The object had a smooth, dull, steel-gray or silver surface, and was shaped like two discs pressed together, the bottom being flatter than the top. Four long legs extended from the underside (Allan remembered seeing only two legs but assumed there were four).*

*The legs extended below the rise along Allan's sightline. As he watched, the object slowly rose vertically. He quickly ran outside but saw nothing more of it. He later found what he called "pod marks" in the clay-like soil near the rise. Only one of these alleged marks was visible the day I visited the site, on April 23rd. The hole was four inches deep, six inches wide at the top and lay on an inclined portion of ground. It lay near a partially buried can. The immediate area is open with a dirt access road running through it. The topsoil has been removed from some of this area; what remains is claylike and dry. The remains of an old hog pen lie atop the rise.*

*I had Allan stand where he remembered the other holes and measured the distances. The result was a roughly rectangular area. Allan's idea was that these distances were the spacing between the four legs of the craft as it rested on the ground. The investigators consider these events to be the most important and best documented. However, a host of attendant events involving both entities and UFOs were reported before and after this period. (61)*

In what sounds like orbs coming out of a craft, on September 17th, 1966 at Cranes Beach in Ipswich Bay, there was a luminous, yellow, cigar-shaped object which emitted smaller glowing objects that moved around independently. (58) The next relevant sighting was on January 15th, 1967 in Greenville, between 5:45 PM and 6:05 PM. There were three successive sightings of discs with ports flying at the treetop level. Witnesses saw light beams that brightly illuminated the ground. They watched the discs hover low with a buzzing sound. On January 18th in South Williamstown, a dome disc with body lights paced a car. There was a power failure in the area immediately prior to the sighting.

January was a busy month. Five days earlier on January 20th in Methuen, while driving her car, Kimberly Dodge noticed a disc in the sky with red lights. There were electromagnetic effects that occurred with her car radio, motor, and headlights. She noticed it moving slowly over a field where it hovered. She noticed two red and two white lights on the body of the craft. The craft then shot away and her vehicle resumed to functioning normally.

On February 10th, 1967, in Worcester around 5:30 PM, an

object with three bright body lights hovered over a house, moved to the south, stopped, hovered and sped away. A color TV faded to black and white, and the contents of the refrigerator froze solid during the sighting. Seven days later, on February 17th, 1967 in Lawrence, there was a v-shaped UFO of "dazzling brilliance" with a variety of body lights. The UFO hovered over the highway. The witness drove under it. There were similar sightings close by in Methuen and Andover at around the same time. (62)

In what resembles the description of orange orbs again, between the 20th and 27thof February, glowing orange or red objects were reported at least five times, typically hovering at low altitude and or pacing cars. This occurred from the east coast to the mountain states. (63)

On April 11th, 1967 in Orange, MA. at 6:45 PM, a flat disc with a red light moving around the underside of the craft, moved slowly then accelerated and sped away. Then on April 19th, 1967, in Tully around 7:30 PM, a white-domed object with body lights was seen flashing white then red. It hovered and made sharp turns.

On April 20th in Bolton, not far from Leominster, with a short drive down Route 117, a domed disc with eight glowing yellow ports around the perimeter was seen. It had various colored lights. It took off with what sounded like the sound of bugs, slowly, then it sped away. (64)

On May 11th, 1967, two officers of the Wareham Police Department watched two objects that looked like inverted dishes. There were lights that rotated around the rim of the craft. They moved up and down and then descended into a cranberry bog. Both then took off at high speed when officers shone their flashlights on them. (65)

It bothered me that I hadn't heard these stories. I began to wonder if our own government didn't know what they were up against at this time. Or if they did, they didn't want to alarm the public. Because for some, this could be too much to handle. There would be utter chaos.

A letter was sent to UFO researcher Raymond E. Fowler from Bryce M. Hand, who was a professor at Amherst College. He was driving north on Route 47 between Amherst and Sunderland on September 23rd, 1967 when at 1:37 PM he noticed a silver elongated object in the sky ahead of him.

He first thought it was an airplane leaving a contrail, but its size (about 10 seconds of arc) was too large, suggesting it was close. Still, he heard no sound. Suddenly he noticed that there was a second object that was similar to the first. It was to the left and below the first object. They were both moving north/northwest on straight parallel lines of travel. Professor Hand, then stopped the car to get a better look at what he was seeing. He didn't notice any wings or tail planes. Within the time of about ten seconds, the objects flew out of view. (66)

It was relatively quiet until March 3rd, 1968 when throughout the eastern and central United States, hundreds of people reported fiery objects streaking across the sky. It was 8:50 PM on the east coast and some of these fiery objects were showering the ground with sparks, leaving bright trails behind. The year of 1975 brought a concentration of UFO sightings in Canada and the Northeast again from July to November of that year.

On June 6, 1974, in South Hampton, a Ms. Vivian Stevens, and her children witnessed a domed object with multi-colored lights as it moved with a bobbing motion. When it descended near the road, the witnesses fled in fear. (67)

Lee Merkel Jr. wrote an article about UFOs on February 6th, 1977, for the *Sunday Worcester Telegram*. The article was referenced in the book *Clear Intent*. There were sightings of black helicopters near UFO sighting locations. These helicopters have also been associated with the cattle mutilation mystery.

*"...1975 through early 1976, Maine, Massachusetts, and New Hampshire – though cattle mutilations have occurred in New England, none were known during this period. However, there were disappearances of smaller animals and the mutilation of fowl, such as geese (and not for the first time. Geese had been mutilated in Colorado in 1975 - scene of the cattle mutilations). Some of the animal owners had seen low-flying suspiciously behaving unmarked helicopters."* (68)

Did all of this attention in central Massachusetts with UFOs draw the interest of the CIA or some government agency? Black, unmarked helicopters have been seen in areas of UFO sightings and before or after cattle mutilations. Could these "helicopters" that people were seeing be the UFOs themselves? Possibly mistaken as UFOs at night due to the hovering lights? Or were these helicopters intentionally pretending to be UFOs, with the intent of fooling the public?

The story of Betty Andreasson seems to have piqued the interest of some government agency after details of their otherworldly encounters were exposed to the public. During the continued investigation of their experiences, while the chief investigator Larry Fawcett was working with Author Raymond E. Fowler, Bob Luca, Betty's husband, was getting fed up. He was continually coming up empty when searching for answers on who was flying these unmarked mysterious black helicopters over their home. A FAA official seemed to think that the likely culprit of the mysterious black helicopters was none other than the Central Intelligence Agency.

*"During the early part of 1980, when Larry Fawcett was working on the Andreasson Affair Phase Two as the chief investigator for author Raymond Fowler, mystery helicopter events plagued both Betty Andreasson and her husband Bob Luca. They reported that their home was overflown numerous times by black, unmarked helicopters of the Huey UH-1H type and that these helicopters would fly over their home at altitudes a low as 100 feet.*

*The Luca's described these helicopters as being black in color with no identifiable markings, which is a FAA violation. They noticed that the windows were tinted black also so that no one could see inside, During many of the overflights, Bob was able to take close to 200 photos of the helicopters. These overflights were witnessed not only by Fawcett but by the Luca's neighbors as well.*

*One letter that Bob Luca sent to the Army's office of the Adjusted Ground, dated, May 8th, 1982, was the culmination of complaints for the previous several years of overflights. After getting negative answers from all agencies connected, Luca demanded a final answer on why the helicopters continuously intruded on his property. He included a comment by a FAA spokesman, who had listened to Luca's description of the flights.*

*The spokesman suggested that the helicopters might belong to the CIA, The CIA later denied that this was possible, but the FAA spokesman's comment was certainly suggestive"*
(69)

Was the CIA was trying to find out who was flying all of these UFOs as well? On January 5th in 1979, three glowing red, triangular objects confronted a car. The vehicle's forward motion was impeded and there were physiological effects upon the passengers inside. At 6:20 AM while driving to her parent's house in Auburn, Massachusetts, Ann Marie Emery saw three red, glowing triangular objects over in the woods to the left of her.

After rounding a corner, Ann was confronted by these three red objects as they were hovering over the road in front of her. Her radio failed, and the car automatically slowed to a stop, with the engine still running. She then felt heat and paralysis and smelled a pungent odor. When another car had approached the objects accelerated upwards one at a time and disappeared. Her radio came back on as soon as they were gone. She suffered a mild rash due to heat effects around her eyes and nose the following day.

On January 26th, 1990 there was a long-lasting fireball/meteor that streaked across the Northeastern sky with a bluish and green color. It had a short tail and changed from white and orange as it broke up. This was observed around 7:50 PM.

On February 23rd, 1990, there was a prominent fireball sighting at about 7:50 PM, where it changed color from white to green to orange. March 4th, 1990, at Woods End in Provincetown, MA, a sphere that contained windows was seen from a boat near a lighthouse. Several objects were observed taking off at high speed with loud booms. It stopped and hovered while flashing bright white lights. (70)

On March 6th, 1991, in the Northeastern United States, from Maine to West Virginia, in the hours of 2:30 AM to 3:00 AM there were fireball/meteor sightings. The fireball/meteors were green and red sparks emanating from them. They moved coming from the east and headed towards the north. (71)

These are just some of the investigated UFO sightings in Massachusetts. After reading through all of these accounts, I had a hard time believing that everyone was lying and making this stuff up. The accounts involving different police officers and educated witnesses were very compelling. UFO sightings continue to occur and they are being seen in Leominster and the surrounding areas.

UFO sightings seem to have increased exponentially the past several years. I believe it is because we all have cell phones now and more and more people have ways of capturing these craft and strange lights on video. These videos can then be easily shared on social media for others to see. It's quite possible that we are heading towards some type of major event as more people are increasingly being exposed to this and other types of strange phenomena.

# BIGFOOT TRACKS?

A casual hike in Leominster State Forest on June 27ᵗʰ, 2010, would suddenly become a life changing event for a Leominster couple. Their story was highlighted on Animal Planet's TV show *Finding Bigfoot* as well as *The Sentinel and Enterprise* and *The Leominster Champion*, both local newspapers. The couple entered a trailhead on the outskirts of Leominster State Forest with the intention of heading down to Notown Reservoir. According to the *Sentinel and Enterprise* article, "they each had the day off and decided to hike through Leominster State Forest even though the temperature was in the high 90's, they figured it would be cooler than lying on the beach."

They entered the trail on Granite Street, its entrance behind Leominster High School. Granite Street is a dead end road that literally ends and the hiking trail begins. There is a small parking lot up to the right once you reach the top end of Granite. The hike to the edge of the Reservoir is about an hour's walk with a steady pace.

The couple was about twenty minutes into the hike. The couple recalled that there were no cars in the parking lot at the Granite Street entrance. They didn't feel like they were alone in the woods that day. Per *The Leominster Champion* article, they noticed that there were no sounds of any birds or wildlife as they were hiking along the trail, just a weird feeling. This lack of wildlife or birds is a commonality prior to and during Bigfoot encounters.

There tends to be an eerie silence and a lack of animal sounds in this immediate area of Leominster State Forest. I have experienced this several times. It is almost as if the wildlife knows when these cryptozoological creatures are around and they suddenly go quiet and start hiding.

As they were walking along, they came to a fork in the trail. According to *The Champion*, "We were just walking and talking, heading up to Notown Reservoir when the path split. I wasn't sure which path to take, so we chose one and started walking on it." They were aware of the extremely muddy terrain just before this fork in the trail, looking as if it were a freshly opened jar of peanut butter. I have been to this spot and this particular section of the trail is smooth and flat with no impressions or rocks. The rest of the trail heading towards Notown Reservoir is full of jagged rocks and sharp edges.

As the couple retold their story on *Finding Bigfoot*, suddenly, as they were about to move along, they both heard what sounded like a grunt. They both stopped dead in their tracks. Whatever they heard, it sounded close. The husband, an experienced hunter, and outdoorsman thought he knew what the sound was and patiently waited for a buck to jump out onto the trail, but nothing happened. "I thought it must have been a deer or something, but it was leaves and branches crunching and breaking. I got a weird feeling and so did my wife." After a few moments in wait, they dismissed the sounds and continued on along the trail.

Within ten or fifteen minutes they realized they were going the wrong way. With the oppressing heat and sweat pouring down, the couple headed back into the direction from which they came.

As they approached the fork in the trail, again coming from the other direction this time, the couple noticed that the stretch of mud that their attention was drawn to earlier, had some indentations on it. "We had just been there, and when we came back there were footprints, with five toes, and at least three and a half inches deep in the mud, they were some serious tracks." They both experienced an eerie feeling and wanted to get out of there.

There were six tracks. All of them appeared as if whatever created them jumped out of the wooded area and onto the trail. There were also deer hoof prints alongside these tracks, yet no sight of a deer in the area earlier. The husband told *The Sentinel* that the tracks were so deep and so far apart it was shocking. "Who would be up there randomly on a Tuesday afternoon running barefoot?" It appeared that whatever made the prints weighed several hundred pounds. They became frightened with the find and the husband quickly picked up a large rock for protection. As they both studied the tracks, they had the sudden sense that they were being watched. "Right where the footprints ended, the deer prints ended so we figured he (a sasquatch) scooped it up."

The sound that they both heard before heading back and discovering the tracks was thought to be some kind of warning noise. The husband recalled to *The Leominster Champion* that he "started to think back to the area in Leominster that was known as Monsterland, and a story that someone went out there and never came out. Kids used to go there to party way back when and I remember stories of things people would see out there. Who knows what was living out there."

The area mentioned as Monsterland was an area around Jungle Road and Route 117 where parents would scare their misbehaving children with stories of creatures walking on their hind legs in the woods.

The couple mentioned that they felt like they were "zapped". They were disoriented and had a hard time finding their way out, taking them twice as long to emerge out of the woods. Some researchers have speculated that Bigfoot might use infrasound to immobilize people and to deliver a wave of fear over them.

Siberian tigers have been known to use infrasound to warn other tigers to stay away from their hunting grounds. As well as using the low-frequency sounds, which cannot be heard by humans, to attract mates. The grunt they both heard earlier could very well have been a warning sound. It is also quite likely that they were being hit with a wave of fear from this potential Sasquatch upon discovering the tracks, which would explain why they felt confused and disoriented.

Finding six footprints in Leominster State Forest, six five-toed barefoot prints in the mud, with no one in sight. One could understand how easy it was for them to be a little terrified, not knowing what made those tracks. We have heard of people going missing all the time in National Forests around the country. The footprints were completely out of place. They didn't see anyone out there while they were hiking. They didn't want to stick around to see what made the tracks. An experience like this begs the question, who do I tell it to?

# WHO'S COMING WITH ME?

The couple that discovered the tracks in Leominster State Forest couldn't shake the feeling that they encountered something phenomenal. A couple of days later, the husband ended up calling his mother to tell her about their experience. He also reached out to his brother.

In a strange twist of fate, I had met his younger brother, a few weeks prior to the couples encounter in Leominster State Forest. His brother and I had a random conversation while we were dropping off our kids at school. If it wasn't for that conversation, I never would have known about their experience.

On our way out of the school together, his brother asked me about my time living in California. I talked with him about living in Los Angeles. I would drive back in the summertime to Leominster and I brought up the fact that I did five road trips cross-country. One of the most memorable and amazing places that I visited was the Redwood National Forest in Northern

California.

I told him how after experiencing the size of those trees, breathing in the pine fresh air (where it felt like you were breathing in breath mints constantly). Having the experience of walking amongst these giants of history, with their glowing aura of prehistoric times, the idea of a creature like Sasquatch existing in this environment made sense to me.

"There are just too many sightings over the years for them all to be hoaxes. It only takes one of them to be real" I said. The brother lost it. He was laughing so hard he was crying. "Dude, you are crazy! Sasquatch?! You mean Bigfoot!?" he said. The laughs continued to roll. I was used to this reaction by now. I explained how it has always been an interest of mine and I try to read everything that I can about the subject.

A few days later he got the call from his older brother explaining what he and his wife had found. The husband proclaimed that he was starting to think that what they found were actually Bigfoot prints. My conversation with his younger brother about Sasquatch suddenly had more meaning to him and he took on a serious tone. He excitedly told his brother "You need to talk to my boy Ronny. He knows all about this shit!" He called me immediately after he got off the phone. We arranged for a time for me to interview the husband.

A day later, I ended up talking to the husband over the phone. He was still audibly shaken now after about a week and a half after the experience, dived right into the story. It had been about ten days since this incident occurred. He was still having trouble sleeping and comprehending what they had witnessed.

All he could do was to keep replaying the event in his mind over and over again. He was still trying to understand the whole scenario. He told me the story as if it just had happened a few hours earlier.

I listened intently, scanning for any signs of deceit in his voice. Although difficult for some to believe the story, I found none. Here is a grown man that has been hunting all his life. He's an outdoorsman. This event scared him so much that it continued to haunt him. He called his mother. Something you wouldn't normally do if you were lying or hoaxing about what had happened. I imagined that if it was me, I would want someone to listen to me too. He spoke with such conviction, his voice still trembling. He was adamant that he would never go back in those woods again unless someone was by his side and that person would have to have a sidearm too.

The tone in his voice when he recounted his experience was one of fear and utter confusion. He obviously was still bothered by the experience. And for him, the human answer just didn't add up. The piece didn't fit the puzzle.

I agreed to join the husband and his younger brother back into the woods to see if we could locate the tracks. The biggest challenge would be if we could even find the tracks since they were now about a week and a half old. The probability was very low that we would even locate them again. I wasn't sure that the prints could even survive the elements since so much time had passed.

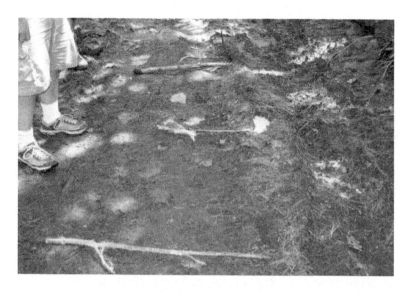

**Author's photos of the trackway**

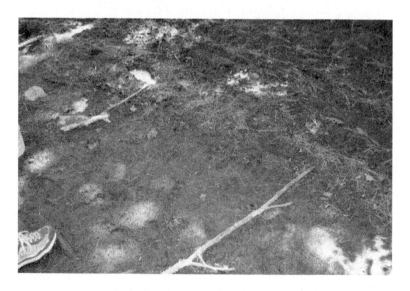

We planned to go back into the woods that Sunday morning. The objective was to go back to the site and see if we could relocate the tracks and document them. As we were closing in on fourteen days at this point, I wasn't feeling very optimistic that the tracks would still be there. I would bring my camera, a Canon Rebel as well as my Taurus 9MM for the husband's sense of peace. In hindsight, if there was something big out there, it was for my peace of mind too.

It suddenly occurred to me that I might be able to cast at least one of the prints if they were still there. My sister Cara had purchased a casting kit, but one that was made for kids. You would mix it with water and then have the kids put their hands or feet down into the mix. This wasn't Plaster of Paris, but I didn't think we would even have the opportunity to use it, let alone find the tracks. I packed it into my bag.

We all met that following Sunday at the High School, taking one car into the Granite Street entrance. As we made our way towards the direction of where the couple found the tracks, the husband seemed to be trying to convince himself that these were no ordinary human footprints that they found. "There is no way in hell there was some person running up this trail and that's who made those tracks. Look at this place! Rocks everywhere! You would cut your feet wide open in just a matter of a few steps if you were running!" he said.

We hiked for about forty-five minutes. The husband, who was leading the charge, yelled that we were getting close. We came to the spot. There was nothing. Disappointed, we continued to search around a bit more and he then realized that it had to be down a bit further. And lo and behold there they were!

I couldn't believe my eyes. I knelt down and when I saw the five visible toes in one of the tracks, the hair on the back of my neck stood up. I got butterflies. I went nuts. I was amazed that the tracks had stayed intact all this time. I called my wife, explaining what I was looking at. It was unbelievable.

I started taking pictures of the prints. We decided that the best-looking print which clearly showed five toes would be our top casting candidate. We knew we only had enough casting material for one. I was kicking myself for not having picked up more material. I also realized that neither of us had remembered to grab some measuring tape. Novices. I looked at the younger brother and he was just amazed as I was. "How in the hell are these still here?" he said.

One thing I noticed right away, the straight line that the prints were in. This is common with Bigfoot trackways. The footprints follow a straight line with an instep. This is very difficult for a human being to be able to pull this off without falling flat on their face. The gait of a Sasquatch is much different from that of a human being. These tracks fit the profile. The stride was impressive. I took out the plaster material and the water and went to work. The brothers started marking the area with sticks so we could label the other prints and we combed the area for other prints or sign.

The husband prophetically said, "We are going to be on National Geographic or something man...on a TV show called Searching for Bigfoot. I am telling you! This is for real!"

We tried to mimic the stride and it was evident that the "thing" was running...and with its bare feet. I just couldn't wrap my head around it. It was difficult to see the deer tracks that were next to these footprints. They seemed to have thinned away. I finally got the casting material to the right consistency so I began to pour in the mixture.

Faintly, in the background, we could hear sounds of engines coming down along the trail. We all looked at each other. The sounds started to get louder. The husband said, "That sounds like a group of dirt bikes or four-wheelers making their way in our direction." The noise got closer and then I could see further along down the trail, a set of four-wheelers that were definitely headed our way at a pretty good clip. I screamed at the younger brother to jump in front of the first footprint that we had just poured the material into. He ran ahead and got in front of one of the four-wheelers with his hands out and directed the two four-wheelers to go around him.

It dawned on my instantly that if we were here another ten minutes later, those tracks would have been toast. They would have been driven over and lost forever. I also realized that if the husband had gone to the beach that day instead of the hike – we all wouldn't be here right now. The find of these tracks was like winning the lottery.

In John Green's book *The Apes Among Us,* the author explained a situation where he was investigating a Bigfoot report that involved footprints. He was confident that he had some genuine prints on his hands. He was a Canadian journalist who was very skeptical in regards to Bigfoot being a real creature. After investigating several cases, he became a believer that Sasquatch does indeed exist. I recalled how Green, filled the prints with plaster and was able to cut out three separate Sasquatch prints out of a dirt road in Canada. Green was worried that the material he was using would not dry properly in time.

"Any of you got a knife?" I asked. The younger brother whipped out a folding knife. "Got one" he replied. I told them both about the story I had read.

**Author's Photo of the Casted Footprint**

"I can't believe that those four-wheelers almost ran over those tracks! It's going to take at least 45 minutes for this stuff to dry." I think we should cut it out of the earth and take it with us." I said. The husband chimed in that we could use the box and slide the track in it and transport it out of here. We did just that. The younger brother got to work and started cutting out the print.

We were beaming with energy and we ran back to the truck in half the time it took us to get out there. We were so excited. I knew deep down that this was something special. I kept asking myself...A Bigfoot in Leominster?

**Author's Photos of Print with visible toes**

For me with the history of the area, and the "time stamp" if you will, with the couple finding the prints several minutes after they were made, and with no other human contact, no one spotted along the trail, makes you wonder what made those tracks. Maybe someone is living in those woods? But then you have the stride length between each of the tracks, which was about six feet. The depth of the tracks, well below three inches deep. You also had the width of the foot which was about half the length of the print. To top it all off, the footprints were in a straight line. These elements coincide with legitimate Sasquatch prints and trackways. What about those deer prints alongside the tracks?

A normal human being has no chance of keeping up with the pace of a deer. They are swift animals and I just can't see a person chasing after a deer, out of their element, especially barefooted! It just didn't add up.

I know that for some, the Bigfoot angle is just too much to handle. Most people will surmise that we have found everything out there, that there are no more new species to be discovered. Not so, the estimated species total is 8.7 million species on Earth! We are still discovering new species every year, about 10,000 of them as a matter of fact. Of the proposed 8.7 million species...we have only successfully cataloged about 3.5 million of them.

A study by the California Academy of Sciences back in 2011 states that "a staggering 86% of all species on land and 91% of those in the seas have yet to be discovered, described and cataloged."

The lead author Camilo Mora of the University of Hawaii and Dalhousie University in Halifax, Canada says *"The question of how many species exist has intrigued scientists for centuries and the answer, coupled with research by others into species' distribution and abundance, is particularly important now because a host of human activities and influences are accelerating the rate of extinctions. Many species may vanish before we even know of their existence..."* (72)

I advised the husband that he needed to put his experience online with a Bigfoot reporting website. At the time and currently, the most recognized and reputable one was BFRO.net (The Bigfoot Field Researchers Organization). I felt that the next step would be to share the experience and see if we could uncover similar stories in the same general area. If there were similar accounts or sightings in close proximity then that would mean we could be on to something. It would only validate the find.

The fact is that we had some solid evidence in my opinion. Even though the size wasn't enormous, they were a decent size and looked much different than a human print. All the prints left behind don't have to be twenty inches long. If they are real, they are having offspring and we could possibly have some juvenile prints.

With UFO and Bigfoot reports, people are reluctant to share their stories. Some will take their experiences to the grave. If these prints were real then I wanted to make it known what was found and where they were located. This is very taboo. It has been a tradition to keep Sasquatch locations top secret.

Every Bigfoot researcher or Sasquatch hunter wants to be the one that discovers Bigfoot. Locations of sightings and track findings are predominately kept secret to keep out unwanted guests, other researchers or people looking to hunt down these "mythical creatures".

But I wanted to create a paradigm shift. Otherwise, when would we ever begin to make any progress? I wanted people to start talking about their experiences. By sharing individual's location of sightings, we would only validate each other's experiences and sightings. Collaboration is the key. The husband agreed to share his story publicly for the world to see and he put it online, filling out a BFRO report. Here's how it lives today on the BFRO website:

**Report #** 28017 (Class B)

Submitted by witness on Monday, July 19, 2010.

Hikers observe and cast possible fresh footprints in Leominster State Forest

**YEAR:** 2010

**SEASON:** Summer

**MONTH:** June

**DATE:** 28

**STATE:** Massachusetts

**COUNTY:** Worcester County

**LOCATION DETAILS:** Leominster state forest, the back side of No Town Res.

**NEAREST TOWN:** Leominster

**NEAREST ROAD:** Route 2

**OBSERVED:** I am 45 years old, have spent my whole life in the woods. I have been hunting and fishing since I was very young. On June 28th my wife and I decided to take a walk in the woods. We were heading to a secluded reservoir located approximately 2 miles in the woods.

We came upon a spot in the woods that seemed liked someone was watching us. We heard a noise come from some bushes. I thought it was a grunt from a buck.

We both expected to a deer come out of the brush. I said, maybe it was a Bigfoot. She told me to shut up and keep walking. We walked for another 15 minutes and realized we were on the wrong path to the lake.

We stopped, ate lunch and headed back into the woods. We had stopped at some power lines and sat in some shade. It was over 94 degrees that day, and this was about noon time.

As we walked back, we both noticed some very DEEP footprints that did not look right. They were clearly 5 toed "Human" prints. In between the prints, there were some deer tracks.

The tracks clearly looked like the Human prints were chasing the deer prints. We both looked at each other and said, why would someone be running barefoot, in 100-degree weather in the middle of the woods on a Tuesday afternoon?

There were no other people in the woods at that time. The tracks were not there the first time we passed this spot, the noise was, but the tracks were not.

At this point, I became very concerned that whatever made the prints was still in the area. I grabbed a big rock and told my wife to take some pictures with her cell phone. The tracks were about 6 to 7 feet apart.

I could tell the first print was a right foot that jumped out of the woods. The sixth and final step was a left foot that looked like it pushed off into the woods. No other tracks were before or after these six prints.

We both became very nervous and started talking loudly

and whistling. I did not want to run into this "person". We became a little confused and ended up on the wrong path home. We walked for a couple hours, no way were we going back the way we came.

Did not notice any smells or sounds. Just very quiet. No animal sound at all.

**ALSO NOTICED:** We took many pictures and made a casting of one of the prints. They were the deepest prints I have ever seen. No doubt a HUGE animal (human) made them. They were at least 3 to 5 inches deep. I did not even make a print when I stepped in the same area. I am 230lbs.

**OTHER WITNESSES:** My wife. Went back to the spot on 7/18 and found the same tracks with my brother and Friend.

**OTHER STORIES:** We did feel like we were being watched the whole day yesterday. No animal sounds, very quiet again.

**TIME AND CONDITIONS:** Prints were found at 1:00 PM EST

**ENVIRONMENT:** Rough trail, prints were in hard mud-looked very fresh, lots and lots of cover, blueberries, and deer tracks. (73)

# PAGING DR. BRAKE

The husband went into work that following morning after posting his report on the BFRO website. He checked his email and was excited to see an immediate reply from Dr. David Brake regarding his case. Dr. Dave Brake, the BFRO Field Investigator assigned to the case is a Ph.D., and owns a Bio-Engineering company in Connecticut.

Since there were no active investigators for Massachusetts at the time, Dr. Brake was investigating the report. The husband felt at ease and confident that he could be taken seriously. Here is a smart guy, a Ph.D., a successful businessman and Bigfoot Investigator willing to follow up on the couple's case.

This email exchange occurred on July 20th - 22nd of 2010. He shared this with me and I continued to be a part of the email thread and conversation:

*If you are the individual who submitted a BFRO report regarding a recent unusual experience (sounds, prints) in the Leominster State Forest can you please contact me? I live in SE CT and serve as a BFRO field investigator for southern New England. The submitted report mentioned cell phone photos of the prints - please forward if available, as well as a photo of the print cast.*

*Kind regards,*

*Dave*

*Dave Brake, PhD*

*BFRO Field Investigator / Southern New England*

---

*Hi Dave,*

*Yes, I am the guy who submitted the report. I still can't believe what we found. The original footprints scared the crap out of my wife and me to the point that we became confused and disoriented. We felt a presence that concerned us both. I have attached some of the photo's I took last night of the cast. As my neighbor said, who grew up in Northern NH, that is no friggin' bear print. Very scary!*

*On the casting print, notice the length between the big toe and the smallest toe. It is almost 3.25 inches or less. I measured my foot, and my small toe was on 1.5 inches shorter than my big toe. It looks odd. Please enjoy the photos. I copied Ronny Leblanc on this email, he came with me on Sunday and helped make the casting. God hooked us up for a reason, and that reason is to find Bigfoot!*

*I created a zip file of the photos, I am going to try and send that. Please let me know if you get it. A few emails to follow.*

*Please feel free to call me on my cell-*

___

*Thanks for the quick response. Several of the cast photos look impressive and are suggestive of a non-human bipedal animal. Notably, the appearance of a flat, rather than arched foot, and the possible presence of a mid-tarsal pressure ridge, though without seeing the tracks or cast in person, it is difficult to say for sure.*

*I need you to confirm the length and ball width of the cast print. It looks to be about 10" in length and 5" in ball width. These measurements are important for estimating the width index (ball width/foot length) which trends differently in sasquatches vs. humans.*

*Your observations on toe length difference are good. However, in cast prints, the ends of the toes often appear to curl inward, which negatively impacts the overall foot length and can be misleading in terms of individual toe length.*

*You did not mention taking any stride or step length measurements when you encountered the tracks. Pls. confirm. The stride is the total length of 3 sequential steps and the step length is the length from 1 point on 1 foot to the identical point on the opposite foot. Again, these measurements can help in ruling out humans. I'm guessing it's much too late to go back and measure, so if you do not have it that's fine.*

*I do have numerous other questions but will wait to call your cell until after you provide any of the information above. I also suggest that you minimize the number of people that you show the cast to as well as a number of people that you share your experience with.*

*I also need to check our database for other submitted, but non-published reports from this general area. I'm also interested in possibly adding your submission to the public database (with your permission; of course all personal information and exact location remains confidential) pending the outcome of a phone interview with you and hopefully, your wife as well since she was also a primary witness.*

*Thanks again.*

*Dave*

---

*Hi Dave,*

*Wow, you are the guy we have been looking for. This is real, I don't care what people say. I will stop telling folks about the tracks. I only showed my brother and Ronny where they were. I am pretty sure the tracks may still be there. I did do some quick measurements of the prints when we first found them.*

*They were about a foot longer than I could fully stretch,*

*which is about 4 feet. I would say they were at least 5 feet apart and all the same length. That was the first thing we noticed was how far apart the strides were, plus how deep the prints were. My wife and I both said, oh my GOD, these prints are not human. They looked like the "human" was chasing a deer. There was clearly deer track in between the footprints. No doubt in my mind, it was on that deer's ass.*

*Six steps, the first one was a right foot that jumped out from the woods. The sixth step was a left foot that went back into the brush. You could clearly see how the "person" pushed off with the left foot to jump into the woods. All six steps were about the same distance apart. I would say he (or she) was running.*

*I have not yet mentioned that we did see what we thought was a CHILD's barefoot print in the area. My wife said, wow look at these little prints. I also had seen them, but could not get a good shot of them with the camera. One photo is of them, but cannot see them very well.*

*They were not nearly as deep as the big prints. I think it was a Mother and child, waiting in the bushes. She made a noise when we passed to let us know she was there.*

*I thought it was a deer grunt and expected to see a deer run by. We also heard a loud" snap" and movement in the bushes when we first passed that area. The prints were found on our way back.*

*When my wife was taking the first set of pictures, we were so scared that I picked up a rock and told her to get the pictures quickly so we could get the hell out of there. We both felt like we were being watched. It almost felt like we were being tricked about our location. We did become disoriented and went out of the woods, via the wrong path.*

*What was a last minute idea to go for a walk in the woods, has turned into something beyond my wildest childhood dreams. I truly feel that GOD put us there for a reason that day. Starting with taking the wrong path to get to the lake. If I would have taken the correct path, we would have never found the tracks. Period. Everything happens for a reason.*

*I have the print, Ronny and I are going to make some more observations of it tonight. We will get exact measurements. The print is 10 ¼ long by just under 5 inches wide.*

*We should be home tonight if you would like to call us. Ronny may also be there tonight around 7:00. Maybe a good time to get all of our stories?*

*Please let us know what we should be looking for. I want to go back out and look some more.*

*How large of an area do you think a Bigfoot would cover? I do know other access points into the area and wonder if we should go to the spot via a different path.*

*I would love to have my story posted, it is real, no bull crap. It is what we had seen. It makes no sense that a huge person would be out in the woods on a random Tuesday afternoon, 95 degrees, playing a hoax on us.*

*All input is greatly appreciated.*

We had a phone conversation with Dr. Brake and I mentioned that there was a blueberry patch, an enormous one directly next to the path where the print was found. He confirmed that there was a recent sighting of something in Ashburnham and Gardner within the last six months. He wrote his follow-up and posted it to the BFRO website under the couples case.

**Follow-Up Investigation Report by BFRO Investigator**

**D.A. Brake (Ph.D.)**

*Both husband and wife witnesses were independently phone interviewed approximately 3 weeks after the reported incident. Both witnesses retold the same story and a 40-minute inquiry provided some additional details summarized below.*

*The couple had previously hiked in this rural area of the state forest numerous times and was somewhat familiar with the secondary trails on which they were hiking. Approximately one hour into the hike the husband heard a loud and distinctive, single 'grunt' from close range followed by very brief heavy footfall movement.*

*The area on both sides of the trail had thick underbrush with no significant visibility. The wife did not hear the vocalization but described the brief movement as 'heavy leaf crunching". The couple remained still and relatively quiet for approximately 30 seconds, and not hearing anything further continued on the trail.*

*Approximately one hour later, about 1:00 PM, the couple was headed back on the same trail. In the same area of the initial vocalization both simultaneously observed a highly visible set of 6 footprints (3 pairs of right-left prints) on the trail in a patch of relatively hard, dry mud. The tracks were headed in the same direction as the witnesses were walking.*

*Both witnesses stated that they did not see the footprints on the trail while stopped earlier on the hike in, and were particularly surprised by both the depth and distinctive toes of the prints.*

*Upon further questioning, the husband stated that a set of fresh looking deer prints were co-located with the footprints, along with a short track of less distinctive but noticeable smaller footprints.*

*The husband commented that he believed whatever left the footprints was 'chasing' the deer since both sets of tracks were co-located and headed in the same direction. While stopped and investigating the prints and tracks, both individuals commented that the forest was unusually still and quiet.*

*After taking cell phone photos, the couple continued on the trail but quickly became uneasy, nervous and disoriented to the point that both reported becoming temporarily lost on the trail network. Both witnesses reported not seeing any other hikers on the trail that day. The original cell phone photos are of relatively poor quality.*

*The witness and two other adults returned to the site approximately 3 weeks later and the witness reported that several of the prints were still visible. A cast was successfully made of a single, right-foot print. Measurement shows print to be approximately 10" length, 5" width, and heel depth of 2.5".*

*This incident took place in a relatively unused portion of Leominster State Forest, a 4,300-acre parcel of forested land that has remained largely undeveloped since Colonial settlements in the early 1700s. The forest is part of an expansive greenway area that includes Wachusett*

*Mountain State Reservation containing the largest known area of Old Growth Forest east of the Connecticut River in Massachusetts.*

*The entire greenway is comprised of upland hardwood forests, alpine meadows, ponds, streams, and wood and shrub swamps. The area supports a rich and diverse wildlife and bird population. The location of these prints is approximately 4 miles northwest of an area in southern Leominster known by locals as "Monsterland", a nickname that originates from purported sightings by numerous individuals of a hairy man on the same stretch of road in the 1950s and early 1960s. This incident is also approximately 15 miles southeast of BFRO Report 8717*

About BFRO Investigator D.A. Brake (Ph.D.):

D. Brake holds a Ph.D. in Immunology and attended the Maine 2008 expedition. (74)

The couples' experience occurred back in June of 2010. It would be almost a full year before the Bigfoot craze seemed to explode on a national level when a certain television show debuted. Dr. Dave Brake had developed a rapport with the couple and he believed their story.

Brake was working with BFRO founder Matt Moneymaker regarding recent cases that they could highlight on the show FINDING BIGFOOT. Dr. Brake asked us if we would entertain the idea of coming to a town hall taping for the new show. They would be in Rhode Island for the day. FINDING BIGFOOT, the show that follows four Bigfoot researchers traveling the world in their quest to prove the existence of Bigfoot, wasn't even on the air until May 30th, 2011. It's currently in its ninth season.

The story was featured on the popular documentary

television series in January of 2012 on the episode entitled "*Big Rhodey*". The husband recounts how having his story aired on the show would never have come about if I hadn't encouraged him to post his story online with the investigative group. We would never have met if I hadn't had that conversation with his brother that day about Sasquatch. I was just happy to be a part of the experience.

We were delighted to be invited to come to the taping of the Town Hall in Rhode Island. There was no guarantee that we would be one of the featured stories on the show. But on the day of the shoot, the husband and I drove down to Rhode Island. I told the husband in the car ride down that we were going to get on the show.

"Who else is going to be showing up with a footprint cast? I just feel like we are right where we are supposed to be right now. Like this was all meant to be. Knowing that we sit in the front row at the town hall with the cast in front of us. They won't miss it. And as soon as they hear you tell your story, we are in."

We showed up at the town hall meeting with the footprint cast as well as the earth that was cut out of the trail. We brought maps of the area and all of the photographs that we had taken at the scene. We sat right in the front row as planned. Once the husband gave his testimony to the team of FINDING BIGFOOT and then they saw that what we brought along didn't look like a normal footprint cast, we were approached by one of the producers directly after the taping.

The cast and crew were on their way to New York first thing in the morning to keep up with their busy shooting schedule. My sales skills kicked in. I explained that we were a little over an hour away in Leominster and that they could head west to New York directly after the shoot. The producer looked at me for a beat. "Wait here." The producer then scurried off, jabbering away into his headset and was back within five minutes. "Okay, we want to come to Leominster and shoot. We need directions and a place to meet. How far away is the spot where you found the tracks?" We explained that the hike could be made in forty-five minutes if we hustled along.

We told the producer that we could easily get permission from the Mayor to shoot in Leominster State Forest. The crew quickly adjusted their shooting schedule for New York and made a trip to meet us off Route 2 in Leominster at a Dunkin Donuts. We then took them up to Granite Street and quickly started shooting the scenes for the episode, including a reenactment.

Even though the weather was monsoon-like during the day of the shoot, raining so hard you felt like you were somewhere in the Amazon rain forest that day, we had a good time. We were excited to be able to share the couples' story. As we got closer to the episode being aired, about six months later, I pushed to get the story in the local newspapers the week before the episode premiered.

My mother proclaims that it must have been "a slow news day", but since the experience happened in Leominster, it was highlighted on the front page for both the *Sentinel and Enterprise* with the caption *"Finding Bigfoot in Leominster?"* and *The Leominster Champion* with an article entitled *"A Sighting Unseen"*. Various Bigfoot and paranormal blogs started to pick up the articles when they went up online.

On the day of the episode airing, I called the husband and said "TV, newspapers, next thing that is going to happen is you are going to be on the Hill-Man Morning show on WAAF. Guaranteed." We both laughed. "That would be awesome", he shouted into the phone. "For a scary experience, this sure has been a fun and unexpected ride!"

We always marveled at the twists and turns along the path and choices each of us made to get to this point. It took a lot of courage for the couple to share their story. You can expect people are going to make fun of you, not believe you and call you a "whacko". The couple firmly believes, as do I, that those prints are of something other than a human. Maybe a human-like bi-pedal creature, like a Sasquatch that has been reportedly seen in these same woods for over a hundred and thirty years.

The likelihood that someone had made these prints along that trail off of Granite Street adjacent to deer prints, with the stride and the depth in order to fool someone into thinking that they were Bigfoot prints is highly unlikely. But of course, it is still a possibility.

One would assume that if they were trying to make Bigfoot prints, then they would have intentionally made them much larger than what the couple found. Fifteen or eighteen inches long would be more convincing. Despite real accounts, today, there are more and more people trying to hoax prints or video in hopes of getting on the show and other shows like it on other television networks. Bigfoot has seen a resurgence in popularity the past five years. Bigfoot is a hot commodity.

The show aired on Sunday night January 8th. Literally, that night, after the episode had aired, the husband received a call from WAAF at his house! It was *"The Hill-Man Morning Show"* on 107.3 FM to be exact. They wanted to interview him in the morning about the episode and his encounter in Leominster State Forest. I don't know why, but I just knew it was going to happen.

It seemed after spending time together and in the forest,

the husband and I had gained some "psychic powers". We were more in tune with everything. He would know when I was about to call him and vice versa. And then we would say things that would actually happen. He called me right after he got the call. "Dude, how did you know that!?" he excitedly screamed over the phone. I asked him right back, "How did you know we were going to be on a TV show, way back when we went back up into the woods to find those prints? What are you psychic?" I said jokingly.

"Are you man? What the hell? You knew on the ride down to the Town Hall that we were going to get the show to come to Leominster. It is strange how everything is falling into place for us with this whole thing like it is all meant to happen!" he exclaimed. "They changed their shooting schedule for us! Bottom line is that Bobo and Matt think it's a real Sasquatch print man! So does Dr. Brake. Tomorrow, more people are going to hear about it. We are getting the word out! It's all coming together, brother! Two years ago, I prayed to God asking him to give my wife and me something to do together. This is what he gave us! I don't know why, but I know it was in response to what I asked for that morning. I just didn't expect any of this!"

We talked about how we were disappointed that the episode didn't reveal the location. The show proclaimed to be somewhere near the Massachusetts border. My assumption on why they didn't reveal Leominster was to keep with the continuity and content of the episode entitled "Big Rhodey". The episode mainly focused on Bigfoot reports in the state of Rhode Island.

We were glad that we went to the newspapers with the story because the details that they included were accurate and the location was revealed as planned. We were a little annoyed that the pictures that were used in the episode were not ours at all! I remarked that it seemed as if they were trying to hide the real facts regarding the encounter. But with the BFRO report and the newspapers, we were confident we had accomplished what we wanted.

# 10

# BIGFOOT AND LEOMINSTER STATE FOREST

There have been numerous skeletons of giants unearthed across America over the past 100 years. They have been found near ancient sites in the United States like the Snake Mounds of Ohio...only to have been hidden away. The book *The Ancient Giants Who Ruled America: The Missing Skeletons and the Great Smithsonian Cover-up* by Richard Dewhurst published in 2014, profiles many cases of these skeletons going missing from over the past 400 years.

They include newspaper articles and photos, first person accounts, state historical records, and illustrated field reports that show how the Smithsonian Institute has been hiding the physical evidence of these giants for over 150 years!

Some of the hair on the heads of these skeletons were

blonde and others had red hair. The skeletons were in excess of nine feet tall. There is a good chance that some of these could be the skeletons of Bigfoots. This could be why people have been unable to find any bones. The ones that have been uncovered could simply be whisked away to some secret hiding place. Keeping the secret of the giants away from the general public.

Just when I started to doubt the significance of the footprint find in Leominster State Forest, the stories started to come in. A gentleman named "Harry" had shared this story. He started with: "I know what made those prints!"

He said that he was driving west on Route 2 in Templeton and had stopped at a rest area. When he pulled back onto the highway he saw a very large gorilla on all fours bent over near the road. He was worried it might go into the road and get hit by a car.

As he watched, the "gorilla" looked at him and then turned, stood up straight and took two steps and disappeared into the woods. He was so upset by what he had seen, that he called the Templeton Police Department to report a gorilla-like animal on the loose. He called the State Police Department as well.

When "Harry" got to his home in Fitchburg, which isn't that far away, he called the Fitchburg Police department to also report the sighting! Seems like an unlikely hoaxer if he is going to call three different police departments. The last thing you want to do is create false reports and multiple ones at that Harry said he will never forget what the animal looked like, a huge gorilla.

I have a little trouble with this one because, first the name, it is quite ironic, but also Harry didn't clarify why he needed to pull over at a rest stop in Templeton when he was somewhat close to his home in Fitchburg a few towns away.

On January 3, 2012, a tow truck driver overheard on his scanner that someone had called 911 and reported a "large hairy man" crossing the street. The sighting occurred at the intersection of Elm Street and Hill Street. Richard's Kennel is located nearby.

They have horses on the property and we were alerted that they also had a colt that was a few months old at the time. Sounds like an incredible food source. Something to note, Richard's Kennel is in the same area that the prints were located.

In August of 2011 at Crow Hill in Leominster State Forest, while mountain biking on the Route 31 entrance, a woman reported to a local fisherman and his daughter that she had seen some kind of wildlife chasing her! The fisherman and his daughter watched as a lady, peddling frantically on a mountain bike, came up to them. She seemed quite frazzled and out of breath.

"Are there any bears in the area?" she asked. The fisherman replied in the affirmative that there are black bears in this region. "What about white bears? That run on two feet!?" The fisherman retold the experience and said that she was trembling with fear, sweating, out of breath and definitely seemed completely spooked. The woman continued to tell the fisherman that "the animal followed her as she rode her mountain bike on the path."

It sounded like the creature was paralleling her. It was keeping up with her speed while she pedaled away on her mountain bike. She remarked that this "white bear was running on two feet. It was crashing through the woods...with no problem at all." She told the fisherman that she will "never be back!" She loaded up her bike in her car and tore out of the parking lot. Whenever hearing encounters like this, I always ask myself, would someone really go out of the way to make up this kind of story? Then act it out? For what benefit? So people will think you are crazy? It wasn't until recently that I had heard several instances of people encountering white sasquatches.

Here's another story of a fisherman experiencing something crashing in the woods. During the month of August in 1995, four friends were fishing by canoe in a pond called Massapog. The four fishermen were near the shore when it started to get dark. They reported that a very large animal came crashing through the woods close to where they were. The animal started shaking the trees and growling at them.

This scared them so much that they paddled as fast as they could to the opposite shore in order to get the canoes out of the water. They described the event as if a giant gorilla was trying to intimidate them from going any closer to the shore. This was confirmed by three of the four people that were fishing that warm summer night.

In 2001, after a summer day of riding four-wheelers in Monsterland, a few friends decided to set up camp and a bonfire in Notown Reservoir. Only two of the friends decided to stay out all night long. The rest had made their way back home. At about 3:00 AM or 3:30 AM in the morning, rocks began pelting the tent, one after another. One of the boys got out of the tent to look around. There was complete darkness. There wasn't a sound. Nothing. He went back inside.

The rocks continued to be thrown at the tent throughout the night. The boys both thought that it had to be one of the other guys trying to scare them. As soon as first light hit, the campers broke down their gear and left immediately. When they got back into town, they went straight to one of the boy's house and asked if it was him throwing rocks at their tent. "Are you kidding me, I wouldn't be out there in the middle of the night by myself. No way. It wasn't me," the boy exclaimed.

The other friend that left confirmed as well that he was fast asleep in bed and had nothing to do with it. The boys that stayed and camped out, vowed that they wouldn't come back to camp in the area of Notown ever again. Rocks being thrown at researchers and normal hikers in the vicinity of Bigfoot sighting locations is very common. What's interesting to note is that no one seems to be hit by these rocks. They land perfectly near them. The actions are meant to scare people away. They also claim that they can't locate or see the source of where these rocks are being thrown from.

In that same area of woods, a father and his son were hunting in 2001. As they were making their way through the forest, they were overcome with this strong odor, "a stench like a skunk but like a wet dog with a flesh-eating fungus", recalled the father. "It was disgusting." As they were walking along the trail a bit further, they found a fisher cat that was laying in the middle of the trail. Fisher cats are notoriously vicious and have been known to attack and kill full grown dogs. The father looked around and found that this was an odd find lying in the middle of the trail. He bent down to observe it more closely.

When the father picked it up, the head flopped down. Its neck was broken. He noticed that the body of the fisher cat was still warm! Upon inspection of the carcass, there were no signs of any puncture holes or blood. He also was stunned that this wasn't the source of the stench. The father, a bit puzzled, tossed the animal off to the side of the trail and he and his son continued on. He was trying to figure out what could have done that. It seemed totally out of place. He mentioned that for the rest of the day hunting with his son, they felt like they were being watched the entire time. Although they never did encounter anything else that day, there was an ongoing uncomfortable feeling that hung over them, to say the least.

A group of neighborhood kids were out in the woods around Massapog area during the summer in 2014. They were trying to make their way through the swamp to the pond. The small group consisted of two fourteen-year-olds and one fifteen-year-old. As they were making their way through the swamp, they saw someone walking away in the distance.

The person was huge. It looked as if the person was wearing a black winter jacket, with the hood up, in the middle of summer! The boys yelled to him..."Hey, mister!" Suddenly, the figure, who didn't turn around or respond to the boys' calls, started to pick up his pace. He continued to walk forward and away from the boys. He never looked back. The man then disappeared into the swamp!

When the boys went to the area where they saw this "man", they were unable to get any further due to the swampy terrain. What made them uneasy was the fact that they didn't notice any footprints were they saw the man standing. Upon this realization, they then ran out of the swamp. One of the boys told his mother about what they had seen. He was extremely upset.

What was odd was that this "person" was wearing what looked like a black winter jacket with the hood up, in summer! What's interesting is the "hood" could be the cone-shaped head of a Sasquatch. The black jacket, actually the hair of the creature.

The question remains if this was a person with a jacket or

someone else. The fact that this 'figure" continued on into the swamp, to the point where the boys couldn't even follow, lends credence to the fact that they may have watched a Bigfoot walk away into the swamp. Could the boys be lying? Of course. Could this be the culprit who made those tracks that the couple had found four years ago?

Whether you are hunting or fishing in and around Notown Reservoir area, encounters with something other than the known wildlife in these woods is occurring, repeatedly. A teacher was having lunch in the breakroom with her other coworkers. They started talking about strange stories and Bigfoot tracks being found in Leominster State Forest.

There was a copy repair man in the break room working on a copy machine at the school. He overheard their conversation and asked if they were talking about the Notown Reservoir area. "Yes, that's where this couple had stumbled upon some very large footprints about a year ago", said the teacher. "Oh boy, I have a story for you. I haven't told this to anyone before" he said. The break room got quiet as everyone started to listen.

The copy repair man, Eric, had been fishing all day with a friend. They had acquired a very large stringer of fish. He said they had an amazing day of fishing. One of the best he has ever had. They were having so much fun that they lost track of time. Well, the sun started to set and they slowly made their way out of the reservoir. The darkness seemed to come quicker than expected. There was very little light as they were walking back in the direction of their car.

Eric told the teachers in the lunchroom that due to the amount of fish they had caught, the stringer with all of the fish had some weight to it. To alleviate some of the weight on their journey back to the car, he had found himself a decent sized branch and then hung the stringer of fish on the end of it and then swung the branch over his shoulder. This beat trying to grip the heavy stringer of fish in his hands.

It was very difficult to see anything ahead of them as they walked along the trail. All the sunlight had now vanished over the horizon. They started to quicken their pace as they were walking along the trail in almost total darkness. Eric estimated that they were still halfway to the car when all of a sudden, out from the darkness, something comes crashing through the bushes from Eric's left-hand side and snags the branch attached to the stringer of fish right out of Eric's hand!

It wasn't knocked out of his hands, it was pulled out of his hands. As swiftly as it appeared behind them and grabbed its prize, it was off and crashing through the brush on the right side of the trail. The theft occurred in less than a second. Eric and his companion didn't turn to look at what grabbed the fish. Terrified, they took off in a full sprint towards the car. Tripping and falling in the darkness all along the path on their way back.

Eric said that it happened so fast and whatever it was that pulled the branch out of his hands so quickly had to be huge. The forest erupted as this thing came crashing onto the trail. He also stated that whatever did this...had hands. Eric remarked that his friend afterward thought that it sounded like it was a large bear.

It could have been a bear, but I would imagine it would have attacked both of them as opposed to snagging the fish out of his hands. But what else could it be? A Sasquatch? At the time, that would be the last place Eric's mind would go as the answer.

Eric told the group of teachers that he thinks he knows

what took the fish now, but at the time, it wasn't even a consideration. Eric stated that he and his friend vowed to never return to that area to fish...they have both never been back. He believes that they had a Sasquatch encounter in Leominster State Forest. He has had a hard time accepting the "bear" theory all of these years. The Bigfoot answer makes sense to him.

In January of 2012, after hearing about the story of tracks found in Leominster State Forest, I was contacted by two brothers who have been out in the same area of woods with the intention of looking for additional tracks or evidence. They found some peculiar tracks and took photos.

They wanted to share them with us. They also reported a few days later after finding these tracks that they heard tree knocks while out exploring during a snow storm. Both of the brothers said that the knocks sounded very close and it stopped them dead in their tracks.

They were confident that they were the only ones out in the area at the time. They didn't see anyone the entire time they were there. This sounded familiar. They also found some very large boulders that looked as if they had been moved in the snow, but there were no signs of tracks around these boulders.

If that wasn't enough, a police officer had an encounter as well. This time, it was a visual sighting. About four years prior, a sergeant on the local Leominster police force had an encounter in Leominster State Forest. After hearing about the couples' story, his own sighting and encounter found its way to me. He had an experience while hunting with a friend by the massive power lines. They entered through the Mt. Elam road entrance.

They were hunting for a few hours and then the hunters

eventually split up. The police officer then witnessed up ahead, a large dark figure who peeks out from behind a tree. The figure then decided to move and exposed itself and walked out along the power lines. It stayed very close to the tree line. The figure was all black.

The officer thought that it was his hunting partner at first, but the figure seemed larger. He was also wondering why if it was his partner, he wasn't wearing his hunter orange. The figure, after walking a short distance along the power lines, walked back into the woods and then disappeared.

A couple of moments later the officer felt a hand on his shoulder. His partner came up behind him, which startled the officer. The officer told his hunting partner that he thought he was watching him walking up along the power lines. The officer was dumbfounded at who he was just looking at.

Due to the enormous size and the way it moved, the police officer now believes that he saw a Bigfoot walking along the power lines that day. Not too far away from where the couple had found their tracks, just over the hill, are those same power lines. And like most of these situations, the officer was having a hard time comprehending what he had witnessed. Now, a smart man of the law believes he saw a Sasquatch in Leominster State Forest.

In February 2012, a group of friends had gathered for a big dinner. The buzz in Leominster and at the dinner table was around the FINDING BIGFOOT episode and a creature being in Leomintser State Forest. The conversation got a bit heated. One of the guests, an avid hunter, and in his seventies laughed off the recent story about a Bigfoot-type creature living in Leominster State Forest.

"I have been hunting in these woods for over forty years. I have never in my life come across anything other than the recognized wildlife in those woods. It's all bullshit. Bigfoot? Please! There isn't anything up there. Don't you think I would have come across it by now?" Almost as if someone was listening to his doubt and disbelief of this being a reality, he would have his own encounter.

The old hunter was out hunting by Leominster Sportsman's Club with a buddy of his. They were walking along a trail when all of a sudden some huge black hairy creature walked across the trail right in front of them! On two legs! It didn't even look at them, didn't throw them a glance, just nonchalantly walked in front of the two hunters across the trail and off to the other side.

They both stood there dumbfounded with their guns shaking in their hands. "It was huge! At least seven feet tall. I would bet about 800 pounds. I believe in Bigfoot now! I got to tell you, I am a little weary of going back into those woods after seeing that", exclaimed the old hunter.

I was told a story about a week after the episode aired from a local Leominster resident. Sarah said that she woke up in the morning and went out to start her car for work. That's when she noticed this single footprint, a barefooted footprint on her driveway. It looked to be about twelve inches long. Now mind you, we were in the middle of winter at this point in January. There was snow on the ground.

She looked around and there were no other prints. "I thought that someone might be playing a trick on me. She lives behind Barrett Park, another access point near Leominster State Forest.

With only one print being found, it was assumed that it was probably just someone trying to freak out Sarah. It was highly unlikely that it was real since there were no other barefooted prints nearby. There were some normal boot tracks near the print. The print was located in a high traffic area which led to the door of the home. It was possible that someone took off their boot and sock and made a single track.

Later on that night, I was at a friend's house testing out some different video equipment, a thermal vision camera, also known as a FLIR and other tools to use in an upcoming night investigation in Leominster State Forest. The plan was to do a bunch of different hikes at night in the state forest and the surrounding areas with this recordable FLIR camera and some other audio recording equipment.

One of the guys, was a ghost hunter and he brought a bunch of his ghost hunting equipment. We were checking out his arsenal when he grabbed something from his bag and held it up into the air. He held in his hands what is called a "Ghost Box" or a "Spirit Box".

There is the belief that spirits manipulate energy in order to manifest. They also need some form or energy to manifest sound. The "Ghost Box" communicates with the spirits through the use of a radio frequency. The ghosts or spirits then use this frequency to communicate with the living.

The ghost hunter set up the Ghost Box as we were all talking about the recent single footprint that was found in the Sarah's driveway. Being a single footprint, we had our doubts and thought it was fake.

The ghost hunter powered up the ghost box. Immediately, and I mean within seconds, the box said four things. "Bigfoot....Footprint....Driveway....Real...." We all just looked at each other in shock. That's when I started to wonder what we were really dealing with. We immediately shut off the device.

# 11

# BIGFOOT IN THE BAY STATE

There are certain areas that seem to be "hotspots" for Bigfoot activity in Massachusetts. These areas also contain their unlikely counterpart, UFOs. Isn't that peculiar? Two well-known areas that contain these phenomena are within Massachusetts. They are the Bridgewater Triangle of southeastern Massachusetts and October Mountain in western Massachusetts.

The Bridgewater Triangle was coined by Author Loren Coleman in his book *Mysterious America*, regarding a 200 square mile area in southeastern Massachusetts. Seventeen towns make up this paranormal triangle. The area has a history of Bigfoot and UFO sightings, flying balls of fire, poltergeists, orbs, thunderbirds, and other mysterious animals as well as the evidence of cattle mutilations. Black unmarked helicopters have also been seen in the vicinity. There was a report of a "Yellow Day" in Colonial times as well as several UFO reports, one of them going back to the year of 1760 when a fireball in the sky was seen over the swamp.

The Freetown-Fall River State Forest, within the triangle, is an area that has attracted cult activity, suicides and ritualistic murders and animal sacrifice. The other high activity area within the Bridgewater Triangle area is the Hockomock Swamp. It means "the place where the spirits dwell". This area, like Leominster State Forest, was once the home of the local Native Americans. The tribe that inhabited the area were the Wampanoag People. They had respect for the swamp and considered it a magical place. The swamp was a source of food for the tribe and they hunted these swamps with respect. They believed that the 'good spirits' in the swamp would guide them to their kill.

The colonists however referred to it as "The Devil's Swamp" and "The Devil's Bowl". There are rumors that people have gone missing never to return. The Native American's also used the colonist's fear of the swamp to their advantage as Hockomock was utilized as a fortress against any invasion by the white settlers.

It is said that due to the unfair treatment that the Native Americans received from the colonial settlers, the Wampanoag's cursed the Hockomock Swamp. The area's "strange activity" is thought to also be associated with the Wampum Belt that was revered by the Wampanoag people. It was lost during King Philip's War, 1675-1676. It is believed that until it is returned, the strange activity will continue. King Philip's War was considered America's first major Indian war and one of the bloodiest in American history.

King Philip's real name was Metacom, leader of the Pokanokets, which was a tribe within the Wampanoag Indian Federation. Metacom was the son of Massasoit, who had helped the first Plymouth pilgrims survive their first winter in New England. Hockomock Swamp was one of the locations where a lot of people perished in the war. Reportedly 173 Wampanoag people either died or were taken prisoner there. It is believed that because of the "negative energy" of the area, it has been plagued with red-eyed black dogs, large snakes and Bigfoot-like creatures roaming the swamp and the surrounding woods.

The Bridgewater Triangle is plagued with murders and suicides. There seems to be a negative energy emanating from the swamp. Leominster has its share of "negative energy" as there were rumors of satanic cults performing sacrifices in the Forest. Leominster was rumored to be the "Suicide Capital of the World" in 1984. Susan Roy, who started a local suicide prevention and support group back then, told the newspaper The Worcester Telegram that, based on hospital reports," at least fifty young people had attempted suicide in the city and surrounding communities in the last six months."

From a *Boston Globe* article in 2005 written by Ross A. Muscato entitled "Tales from the Swamp" he writes:

> In his book "History of the Hockomock," local wildlife and conservation journalist Ted Williams wrote that, during the Ceramic (or Woodland) Period from about 300 AD to Colonial times, Native Americans depended on the swamp as an abundant source of game, and also worshiped it. "Hockomock" referred "not only to the evil spirits that struck terror" into the hearts of the colonists, Williams wrote, but also the "good spirits that led Indian to moose and deer."
>
> Over generations, many have believed the Hockomock is home to spirits, strange animals, and more. Stories abound: There are the vicious, giant dogs with red eyes seen

*ravenously sinking their fangs into the throats of ponies; a flying creature that resembled a pterodactyl, the dinosaur that could fly; Native-American ghosts paddling canoes, and glowing somethings hovering above the trees. There's also talk of a shaggy half-man, half-ape seen shuffling through the woods.*

*Students of the paranormal have speculated that negative and disruptive energy was created when the Native Americans of the region were so horribly persecuted and that that energy continues to circulate in the Hockomock. There have been reports of cult and satanic rituals conducted in the swamp. Some believe the Hockomock Swamp is cursed. (75)*

October Mountain, which contains the largest state forest in Massachusetts, has its share of strange hovering lights, mysterious big cats, and Bigfoot creatures. UFOs are yet again in the mix. An early Bigfoot report from Massachusetts comes from the North Adams area of October Mountain in August of 1861. Search parties had shot at a gorilla looking creature during this time. Just over the border in Bennington, Vermont, also referred to as the Bennington Triangle, there were sightings of this "hideous" gorilla around this time as well. (76)

The reason the area gets its name, "The Bennington Triangle" is because, well you guessed it, it also has UFO sightings, strange lights in the sky and Bigfoot encounters. Remarkably, the area is also considered by the Native Americans of that region to be cursed. Just like the Hockomock Swamp.

In July of 1909 in Haverhill, Massachusetts, police in the city were searching the wooded area which reached the border of New Hampshire. Around Gile Street in Haverhill, the police looked for a "mysterious wild man" that was seen. (77) There were sightings of Bigfoot throughout New England and New York for decades after this. There was also the occasional hoaxer as well. A Bigfoot hoax sighting took place in late December in 1976 in Agawam, Massachusetts. A sixteen-year-old boy confessed to creating twenty-seven inch long human-like footprints in a wooded area of Agawam when the National Media focused on the story and the area. (78)

Due to privacy and fear of ridicule, most reports have a lot of details missing from them, like precise locations as well as identification of the person or persons reporting the experience. Most of the time, the names of the individuals are withheld. You can understand why someone would not want to reveal their identity. A lot of researchers will automatically assume that the person isn't being forthright if they won't come forward and will more often times than not, dismiss the case as a hoax. In December of 1977, snowmobilers had a close encounter from about fifty feet away.

A father, his son, an uncle and several friends went up to a cabin owned by a hunter's club on Old Colony Road in Gardner, Massachusetts. It's an area that is close to Leominster, to the west with the location in central Massachusetts. The sighting took place on the edge of a swamp and very close to some old train tracks that run through the area. They had a sled attached to the back of the snowmobile and they took turns driving it around. If you were not driving then you would be standing in the sled on a footrest. Their plan was to spend the night at the cabin. After they had dinner, the son decided to go with one of his friends and take one of the snowmobiles before darkness arrived:

*"It was about 4:00 PM, or so, it was just getting a little dark. My friend and I left the cabin with the snowmobile, he was driving first and I was on the footrest on the sled. We left*

*and came up to the swamp, crossed over the tracks and headed down the road about 50 feet or so. It was getting a little late and we decided not go too far so we turned the sled around on the road. We had to pick it up because of the narrowness of the road. Once we turned it around it was my turn to drive.*

*So now we were facing the tracks and the swamp is on both sides of the road. The road goes right through the swamp and the tracks cross right by the edge of the swamp.*

*At this point I looked behind me to see if my friend was on the sled and holding on, when I looked up I saw this creature walking on two legs like a human. He crossed right by the tracks at the edge of the swamp and crossed the road right in front of us. I remember it looking at us and I remember the arms swing clearly...I remember its size, that's what was scary, so large, I'd say about seven to nine feet high, weight about 400 to 500 pounds. At least for something that size it would most likely be heavy. I know the woods there well. I've spent years in the military and hunt every year. I have been trained in tracking and survival in the woods so I know what I am saying and what I saw. But the thing took about two steps and he was across the road. All black hair didn't notice any smells, but I can tell you this. I won't forget that day ever.* (79)

On April 13th in 1978, a Bigfoot was spotted crossing the road in the Parker River National Wildlife Refuge on Plum Island. The Refuge road is over six miles long and comes to a dead end. Two guys and two girls decided to take a ride and went to the observation tower located on the refuge. Details of the witnesses' names and ages are not available. The driver of the vehicle, Rich, reported the sighting. His male passenger, Eddy, was sitting up front. The four of them got to the end of the road and they decided to go up and explore the observation tower.

After about thirty minutes of being there, Rich said that he could hear loud clicking noises from their location in the observation tower. Then he started to hear short high pitched screams coming from about one hundred yards away from their position. He looked around but didn't see anything and then made a mental note that there were no birds or people around anywhere. After the "lack of sounds" continued for about another ten minutes, he became very uneasy and encouraged the others that they should leave.

They got into his car and started the drive out of the refuge area. They got to about two miles down the road, when a large dark figure emerged from the marshland on the left side of the road, crossed the road in three steps and then exited on the right side of the road and into the solid brush and disappeared. Estimated to be about seven feet tall, all black from head to toe, the creature moved across the road with its arms swinging, hunched over, but with great ease and smoothness. The sighting lasted for only a few seconds when Rich turned to his friend Eddy and asked: "Did you see that!?" Eddy, replied "Yes!" The girls in the back of the car were talking and didn't see what the boys did. (80)

One area within the Bridgewater Triangle that is purported to have had a majority of the Bigfoot sightings is The Hockomock Swamp. There is an area on the edge of the swamp known as Clay Banks where one of these sightings of a creature occurred in 1978, the same year as the above-mentioned story.

Joe DeAndrade, a former security guard from Bridgewater, was standing by a pond when he felt the sudden urge to turn around. When he did, about two hundred yards away he spotted a brown hairy creature that looked half-ape and half-human. It was making its way into the woods. Joe took off from the area immediately. He didn't stick around. He said that the creature *"was walking slowly, like Frankenstein, into the brush."* (81)

There was an incident in the area in 1970, where a Bridgewater resident complained to the local police that he saw an upright, bipedal hairy creature that was ripping through the woods and backyards of his neighborhood. There were several inquiries by the police looking for the culprit. One of the officers decided to stake out the place and while he was waiting in his patrol car, the vehicle was picked up off the ground! He turned around with his flashlight and pointed it towards the rear of the car and he witnessed what looked like a bear running away on two legs. They later found tracks after another sighting report.

In the town of Mashpee in Cape Cod, Massachusetts, two men reported seeing a tall creature covered with dark fur and walking on two legs. They said that the creature was accompanied by a black dog. This occurred around 3:00 AM in the morning in front of a garden center on Route 151. This friendly interaction with a Bigfoot and a dog is rarely seen. Most of the time, people report their dogs going missing or that they are so terrified that they will not pursue or go after a Bigfoot, but will cower and run away. (82)

In 1983, a fur trapper by the name of John Baker was canoeing in a river that is adjacent to the Hockomock Swamp. He was setting muskrat traps on this chilly winter night when he suddenly heard a loud crashing sound of something running through the nearby woods. He had been trapping in this area for over thirty years and never encountered anything like he was about to see. He then turned towards the noise, curious as to what was making the sounds. He then spotted a huge hairy creature, which entered the river with a splash and passed within yards of his canoe. He smelled a musky, skunk-like odor. He never encountered the creature again. (83)

That same year in another area known for Bigfoot activity, October Mountain, two men had a Bigfoot sighting on August 19th. The next day, Monday, the men walked into the office of the Berkshire Eagle to report their strange encounter. Eric Durant was eighteen at the time and Frederick Perry, twenty-one. The two were having a cookout with a couple of their friends. They started to hear strange noises around 10:00 PM.

These strange sounds continued on until about midnight. Both Eric and Frederick then got the courage to try to find the source of the noise. About a hundred yards from the camp, they could see a huge outline of a creature about fifty yards ahead on the trail. Their headlights illuminated the creature in the bushes, which stood seven feet tall, had dark brown hair and strange glowing eyes. Standing on two legs, the creature didn't look as if it could be a bear. It quickly vanished as Frederick got out of the vehicle and started to walk towards it. Despite the fact that this was something that sounded like a very scary experience, Frederick claimed that upon looking at the creature, he got the impression that *"whatever it was it didn't look like it was going to harm you."* (84)

In 1989, a hiker, who was also a bear hunter, had a much more detailed sighting of a Bigfoot creature in the Berkshire Mountains. He reported his encounter to the local game warden, who suggested that the creature was probably a bear or a moose. After his experience, he wouldn't go back into the area unless he had a hiking partner and a rifle in his hands. The encounter can be found in the book *Bigfoot Across America:*

*"I observed a slight glimpse of a moving object about 100 yards ahead of me...At first, all I could see was arms moving*

*and an occasional glimpse of a fur-covered body...I thought I was looking at a large black bear. I pulled a pair of 40-power binoculars from my travel pack...At one point the animal moved into a clearing. It was then that I realized I was observing something very unusual. The animal was very tall...and slightly stooped. Its body was massive and covered completely with reddish hair...the head was also very unusual in size and shape. The head was rather pointed and covered with hair or fur. The face was dark in color and had less hair than the top of the head. The neck seemed to be non-existent.*

*At that moment, it turned toward me, and I was absolutely shocked. It looked very human...I continued to study the animal...it seemed...Very occupied. It was moving stones and small pieces of wood and grabbing for either roots or insects. I would see its large arm moving to its mouth every so often. What really took me by surprise was that it was stacking them after moving them...At this point, I wanted to get a little closer to see if it was a man in a fur coat or a monkey suit. I was able to get about twenty yards closer. I found a good observation area and studied the animal closer...there he was. Standing right out in the middle of the field. This thing was big. I would say at least nine feet. Maybe less, maybe more because I didn't stick around long to do any measuring.*

*The whole body was covered with hair...Kind of grayish color...that face, I couldn't make...out too good...the hands were like yours or mine, only three times bigger, long legs and long arms. It was like a gorilla...it would make your hair stand up. After a few minutes, the creature ran into an adjacent swamp on two legs"* (85)

In 2004, three hikers were climbing to the summit of Goat

Rock near Stoughton, Massachusetts in November, when they noticed a very bad smell. Then they watched in shock as a large, hairy creature dragged a deer carcass behind him. (86)

In 2009, within the Bridgewater Triangle, a couple was driving on Route 140 along the New Bedford and Freetown lines. It was the middle of July and it was around 11:00 PM in the evening. The girlfriend, who was in the passenger seat of the jeep, saw a hairy man stand up from a crouched position on the side of the two-lane highway. She let out a scream that caused the driver, her boyfriend, to look in the direction she was staring at in disbelief. They remarked that he moved with the fluidity of a man but had ape-like qualities about him. They ended up calling 911 and were told by the dispatcher that they had received several calls regarding the creature between exits 7 and 8 of Route 140. They were sending State Troopers to investigate. (87)

About six months earlier in January of 2009, in North Dartmouth, which is about fifteen miles away from the Bridgewater Triangle, a set of large barefoot prints were found in the snow. A federal law enforcement agent was called to review the curious footprints. His cousin, the owner of the property where these footprints were found, called the agent due to his interest in the subject of Bigfoot. I had the opportunity to meet with him at the *Finding Bigfoot* town hall in Rhode Island. The cousin's daughter discovered the peculiar tracks in their backyard. The tracks were five-toed and looked like a human being's barefoot. There was snowfall about a day and a half prior to the discovery of the prints. From the direction of the tracks, it showed that the creature walked through several adjacent properties, stopping at trash cans along the way before heading back into the woods.

The trackway was witnessed by several family members.

There were photographs but no measurements taken by the officer. He did take a photo of one of the prints with his boot next to it for comparison. The owner of the property remarked how his three cats tend to stay outside. The night before the prints were found, they wouldn't leave the house and were acting strangely. The area has had other sightings of a similar creature. The officer recalled an incident that occurred in the neighboring city of Westport when he thought he saw a Bigfoot going after a family dog. (88)

# 12

# THE ORANGE ORBS

My first orange orb sighting involved two of them flying together, one orb a little ahead of the other, in Leominster. It was in December of 2011. The simplest description would be that they look like little suns. Imagine the setting sun, with that deep orange color. They are basketball-sized reddish-orange orbs made of what it looks like some sort of plasma. They were just nonchalantly moving along from the left of my vision, over my car and then kept going until I lost sight of them.

The orbs looked like they were alive. They moved in a slow, silent manner. Completely silent. Sometimes they are seen at a very low altitude. People are quick to surmise that these are just lanterns. These were not "Chinese lanterns". That was not what I was looking at. I have seen lanterns before. This, I have never seen before in my life. It took my breath away. They were so low, low enough for me to see that I would say they were about one hundred to two hundred feet above my car!

I was driving home from my job in South Boston as the Director of Digital Advertising for the Boston Herald. It was an exciting time for me. I wasn't enjoying the commute to work every day from Leominster to Boston, but loved the work and the people I worked for and with. My birthday was around this time and Christmas was just around the corner. The premiere of the FINDING BIGFOOT episode was airing on Sunday, January 8th, 2012.

I was on Route 2 heading west when I got off at the Mechanic's street entrance. I was heading in the direction of the entrance to the Whitney Field Mall, which was on my right-hand side. As soon as I went through the first set of lights by Nashua Street, I noticed two orange basketball-sized orbs to my left, coming from the south. They were flying over the road and heading north towards Massapog Pond in Lunenburg.

When I was looking at them, I couldn't understand what I was looking at. I rolled down my window and aside from the surrounding vehicles, it was totally quiet. The weather, freezing cold. I wanted to pull over so bad but there was nowhere to do so without causing some kind of accident. The cars traveling so close behind me. I remember the "thought" I had when I was looking at them. I knew deep down inside that I was looking at something that wasn't from "around here". I knew that there was some type of intelligence behind these things as well. I can't explain how I knew, I just did. I knew that what I was seeing was very important.

I came to the other set of lights where the Fidelity Bank building is on my left-hand side. With the light turning red, I reluctantly brought the car to a stop. With one of those after the moment thoughts, I wished I had taken a right at those lights and pulled over to get out of the car to watch them fly away. I faintly noticed the orange orbs continuing on their path and to me, I felt like I was the only one seeing this. I was so excited and I couldn't wait to tell someone.

I arrived home about ten minutes later. I excitedly told my

wife what I had seen as soon as I walked into the door. I sat down at the computer a short time later and pulled up Facebook. I noticed that a friend of mine, Ryan Mullahy was online at the time. Something had compelled me to send him a message. Why? I knew that Ryan had a similar interest in the topics I was into like the mystery of UFOS and the like, based on what I had seen him share on his Facebook feed. What I didn't know is that he was more involved than I expected. Synchronicity some would say.

I sent him a message and simply stated, "Ryan, you are not going to believe what I just saw a little while ago. Two orange balls of light! They were silent and they flew right over my car!" I then thought to myself, "This dude is going to think I am crazy". I could see that he was typing a response. His response came a few seconds later. "Man, YOU ARE BLOWING MY MIND! Were you near the Whitney Field Mall entrance about twenty minutes or so ago?"

I fell back in my chair. The hairs on the back of my neck stood up at attention. I had "goosebumps" all over. He then continued to type another note as soon I replied in the affirmative that I had been there at exactly at that time. "How did you know?!" I typed. He said that "He was leaving work at "City Music" and he was to my right sitting at the lights about to make a left-hand turn to get onto Route 2.

He was on the right-hand side at the entrance to the mall, where I wished I had taken that right to watch the orbs fly away. This was nuts! How the heck would I have known to send a message to someone that saw the same thing? I didn't have to even tell him the location and the time, he filled that in for me before I even had a chance!

He told me he wasn't sure what they were but they sure as

heck were not "Chinese paper lanterns". We decided to set up a time to grab a beer and talk about it further. I was shocked when he told me that he is an independent UFO researcher and has been putting all of his focus on the New Hampshire-based UFO cases! He would later speak on a panel of experts regarding the Betty and Barney Hill Incident at the Exeter UFO Festival in 2014 with Richard Dolan and Peter Robbins.

I was astonished, to say the least. I considered myself "well read" on the subject of Bigfoot and UFOs and I felt that there was definitely a reason for us to see these orange orbs together and to connect in this way. Deep down inside I felt that these orange orbs were connected to UFOs and maybe even Bigfoot. I didn't know how or why, but the synchronicity here was uncanny. There was a connection. I continued to follow the trail down the path of the weird.

Current scientific wisdom states that the luminosity that people are seeing flying around in the sky is not of an alien nature. The orbs are just caused by gas ionization triggered by piezoelectric effect in quartz-bearing rock. Piezoelectricity is the electrical charge that accumulates in certain solid states of matter in response to applied mechanical stress. There is also the "Tectonic Strain Theory" which states that tectonic pressures along fault lines where quartz is prevalent in the local rock create conditions where piezoelectricity is then generated. An electromagnetic discharge is then released in the form of orbs called "earthquake lights' or "ghost lights".

"Ball lightning" is also one of the answers scientists use to explain the mystery of the orbs, but I don't believe it is a correct one. Not for what people have been seeing as of late. The definition for ball lightning is that they are glowing orbs that occur during thunderstorms after lightning strikes. They glow like 100-watt bulbs and they may be white, blue, red, yellow or orange in color and their sizes vary between that of a golf ball to a beach ball. What doesn't work for me with this "Ball lightning" theory to explain away the orbs is that people are seeing these strange lights during normal weather. So if ball lightning is only produced during lightning storms, what exactly did Ryan and I witness?

Becky, daughter of UFO abductee Betty Andreasson, had an encounter with one of these orange orbs. She was just west of Leominster. The encounter occurred in Westminster, Massachusetts. She was about eight years old at the time and it was around the year 1964. One night she woke up to see a glowing yellow-orange ball hovering outside her bedroom window. The object had directed a narrow beam of light at her. Becky screamed and her mother ran upstairs but the orb had vanished. Shortly after this period, Becky developed the ability to automatically write page after page of strange symbols. There was a practice called spirit writing by the early religious Shakers. Becky's script was very similar. (89)

In the book *Incident at Exeter* by John Fuller, he describes that some of the UFOs that were sighted at this time in New Hampshire and Massachusetts were orange balls of light. A Mrs. Edward Liscomb described seeing one of these orbs. "The one I saw last night was a big, orange ball. Nothing but orange."

The description of the undeniable orange orb phenomena screams out again from another UFO sighting that John Fuller uncovered in Massachusetts. "I've seen an Air Force plane chasing one, "a teenaged girl told Fuller. She stated that she was in North Hampton, it was before dark, and the sun had just barely started to go down around 7:00 PM. There were several witnesses to the event as well. It was light enough that everyone could see this jet clearly tearing across the sky. The girl then states that "Just ahead of the plane, was this orange-red ball, like a red ball of fire, and they were both tearing across the sky. And the plane couldn't get anywhere near it." (90)

The Author Terry Ray, of the Book, *The Complete Story of the Worldwide Invasion of the Orange Orbs,* has a theory on what the orbs are and who might be behind them. Terry is a trial lawyer and former United States Air Force pilot.

Terry, on July 29th, 2013, had his own sighting of eight orange orbs, over the course of ninety minutes, while he watched from his hotel room's oceanfront balcony in Ocean City, Maryland. He was on a family vacation, and just couldn't let go of what he witnessed.

They all followed the same path and were flying against the wind. They seemed to be under intelligent control. He had the same feeling I had when he saw them, that they were significant and not from around here. Where others are quick to announce that these orange orbs are just "Chinese lanterns". Terry knows otherwise not only for being a former Air Force pilot but he is also a UFO investigator.

Terry is a MUFON investigator. He came about writing his book and focusing on the orange orb phenomena when he became frustrated with his fellow investigators at MUFON who wouldn't take his experience and sighting seriously! He was facing adversity even in a place that is supposed to be researching these types of things!

After this reaction, he decided to go on a quest to uncover the truth about the orange orbs. He spent over a year focusing on just the MUFON data regarding the orange orb sightings. After researching for over a year specifically on red/orange spherical sightings, utilizing the MUFON database of sightings, he discovered something quite fascinating.

Between 1890 and 1969, there were only eleven orange orb sightings in the United States per the MUFON historical archives. All of the eleven orb sightings were clustered between 1946 and 1969.

One orb was sighted in the 1940's, three in the 1950's, and seven in the 1960's. Then he did a search between 1969 through 2002 and found that there were one hundred and thirty reports. Most of the years in this set had about four sightings per year. The years that stand out are 1997 with nine, ten in 1999 and eleven in 2002.

He then noticed a considerable increase in the sightings over the course of selecting the ten-year span of 2003 and 2013. When he did a search for just reddish-orange orbs (spheres), between the years 2003-2013, there was a total of over 2,225 orange orb sightings *reported* to MUFON in the skies of America! Massachusetts came in at #26 in regards to total sightings out of all the 51 locations that were researched (D.C was included as #51 with only 1) with 33 total orange orb reports. (91)

Terry was a guest on the online radio show, *Grimerica*, which was recorded on January 31st, 2015, and he believes that there are probably a thousand times as many unreported sightings, just simply due to ridicule and scrutiny one would get when sharing their experience. I believe it.

On top of that, he only selected the reddish-orange and spheres as his filters for his search within the MUFON database. As we will find out, the color of the orbs can change and depending on how someone reported their sighting, it may have been classified differently. He now believes millions of people are seeing these things.

Terry also goes on to say that he believes that these orange orbs are out there to be seen! The appearance of the orbs first really starting picking up in the 1940's. During the 1950's, they were around and near sites of nuclear weapons. The big ones are normally orange/red and the smaller ones, which are the size of a basketball, are the unmanned drones. These are the type of orange orbs that get close to people. Some people have had similar experiences with these smaller orbs coming right up to their face. If you remember Betty Andreasson had a small marble-sized orb actually communicate with her when she was in Leominster. The witnesses have explained having the feeling that they were being scanned. (92)

The biggest night when these orbs show up is right after the 4th of July. The second biggest is New Years Eve. Why are these the biggest times? The simple answer, we are focused on the sky. This is the time when fireworks are on display and we are all looking up. Terry thinks that's why they show up. They want to be seen by the masses. In his book, he provides a map of all the sightings across the US. He noticed a correlation with sightings in populated areas by comparing the sightings with a night time satellite photo. (93)

The months and years that I had my sightings were December 2011, January of 2012 and the summer of 2015. There were six orb sightings in 2011 and thirteen in 2012 for Massachusetts. I didn't share any of my sightings with MUFON. When I thought about it, I realized that three of my sightings were around New Year's Eve. The most recent one in 2015 when I saw three of them. I was with multiple witnesses and we viewed them through binoculars at dusk while attending the Starburst Event in Leominster this past June. We were there to see fireworks!

It was still somewhat light out and there was no firework smoke to contend with for good visibility of the sky. It was quite clear. There was a stage that everyone was facing where they had music playing and people speaking. We noticed the first light. The lights seemed to fly by behind the crowd high in the sky buy low enough for us to notice it.

We were waiting for the fireworks and then one of my kids, Aysia, noticed the weird light in the sky behind us. It looked like an orange orb. I got excited and brought my binoculars, subconsciously now I think for this very reason. Too bad, I didn't bring a camera with a telephoto lens. The orbs flew in one by one with a few minutes of lag time in between. They all followed the same flight path like there was some invisible line that they were following.

There were only three of them. We watched the last one approach. We watched it fly by and it vanished in front of our eyes. What's crazy is that I watched it disappear while using binoculars. I was watching through the binoculars and I was following tightly on the ball of light. The orange orb, for a lack of a better way of explaining it, went behind a wall in the middle of the sky. You just couldn't see it anymore. It vanished. It didn't seem to fade out, it just suddenly disappeared. The same type of exit highlighted in previous UFO and orb sightings.

If it was a Chinese lantern, the candle would go out and the paper bag of the lantern, whether it was white or brown would be left floating in the sky. There was nothing there. My friend who was standing next to me stood with his mouth open and was shouting "Where did it go!? Did you just see that? It just disappeared while we were watching it!"

He ran over to his wife and explained what happened. He would call me a few days later saying he posted something on a Facebook site for Leominster asking if anyone had seen the lights. Someone responded that they had seen people lighting off Chinese Lanterns from Hannaford's Supermarket not too far away. He was satisfied with that answer, I, however, was not.

I reminded my friend that looking through the binoculars we would have seen these "Chinese lanterns". That is not what I saw. And how could you explain this lantern just disappearing in front of our eyes? We didn't see the bag go up in flames or anything fall from the sky. This experience got me more inquisitive. I was curious if there were any orange orb sightings that had occurred in and around Leominster in the distant past.

According to Terry Ray, there were only three sightings of the orange orbs for all of the 1950's. If this isn't one of the three sightings, then I am quite astonished that it happens to be in our area. I believe that I may have found another sighting to add to that list from the year 1952! This sighting was reported by several members of the military who actually watched eight of these orbs fly over Fort Devens Army base, a stone's throw away from Leominster!

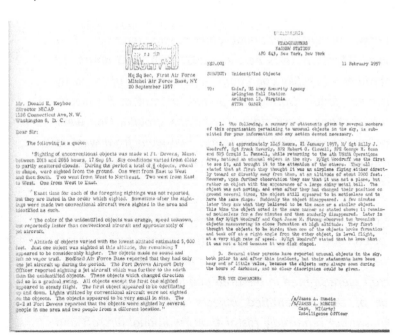

149

This is a letter sent to the UFO Director of NICAP Donald E. Keyhoe on February 11th, 1957 by Captain James A. Muncie of Air Force Intelligence. Donald E. Keyhoe wrote the book *"Flying Saucers Are Real"* in 1950. This was a big move for a military man to come out and say that the phenomena were indeed real. Military witnesses and others reached out to Keyhoe with their experiences. This letter was included in the book *UFO Evidence* compiled by Richard H. Hall and published in 1964 by NICAP. This letter also contained an unclassified memo from Captain Muncie to the US Army Security Chief in Arlington, Virginia. It discussed the events that occurred on September 21st of that same year. I have read about this in another UFO book by author Jenny Randles. But a certain detail has been altered. This letter clearly states eight orange orbs, but Jenny refers to these orbs in the book as "discs". Why? I asked myself. Was this intentional or just an oversight? Seems like a very important detail to ignore.

The following from this letter is a quote:

*"Sighting of unconventional objects was made at Fort Devens, Massachusetts between 2015 and 2055 hours, 17 September 1957. Sky conditions varied from clear to partly scattered clouds. During the period, a total of 8 objects, round in shape, were sighted from the ground. One went from east to west and then south. Two went from west to northwest. Two went from east to west. One from west to east.*

*The exact time for each of the foregoing sightings was not reported, but they are listed in the order which sighted. Sometime after the sightings were made two conventional aircraft were sighted in the area and identified as such. The color of the unidentified objects was **ORANGE**, speed unknown but reportedly faster than traditional aircraft and* *approximately of jet aircraft.*

*Altitude of objects varied with the lowest altitude estimated at 5,000 feet. Just one object was sighted at this altitude, the remaining appeared to be considerably higher. The objects made no sound and left no vapor trail. Bedford Air Force base reported that they had only one jet aircraft up during the period.*

*The Fort Devens Airport Duty Officer reported sighting a jet aircraft which was further to the north than the unidentified objects. These objects which changed direction did so in a gradual swing. All objects except the first one sighted appeared in steady flight. The first object appeared to be oscillating up and down. Lights utilized by conventional aircraft were not sighted on the objects. The objects appeared to be very small in size. The G-2 at FT. Devens reported that the objects were sighted by several people in one area and two people from a different location.*

*1.The following is a summary of statements given by several members of this organization pertaining to unusual objects in the sky, submitted for your information and any action deemed necessary.*

*2.At approximately 1045 hours, 21 January 1957, M/SGT. Bill J. Woodruff, Sgt. Frank Haverly, SP2 Robert O. Clewell, SP2 George R. Dean and SP3 Gerald L. Fennell, while returning to the 4<sup>th</sup>*

*USASA Operations Area, noticed an unusual object in the sky.*

*M/SGT. Woodruff was the first to see it and brought it to the attention of the others. They all stated that at first, they thought it was an airplane flying either directly toward or directly away from them, at an altitude of about 2,000 feet. However, upon further observation, they saw that it was not a plane, but rather an object with the appearance of a large shiny metal ball. The object was not moving, and even after they had changed their position on the ground several times, the object still appeared to be motionless and to have the same shape. Suddenly the object disappeared. A few minutes later they saw what they believed to be the same or similar object. This time the object acted in the same manner as stated above; it remained motionless for a few minutes and then suddenly disappeared. Later in the day, M/SGT. Woodruff and Capt. Jesse M, Strong observed two brownish objects maneuvering in close formation at high altitude. They first thought the objects to be birds; then one of the objects broke formation and took off at a right angle from the other object, in level flight, at a very high rate of speed.*

*M/SGT. Woodruff stated that he knew that it was not a bird*

*because it was disc shaped.*

*3. Several other persons have reported unusual objects in the*

*sky, both prior to and after this incident, but their statements*

*have been hazy and of little value, because the objects were*

*always seen during the hours of darkness, no other clear*

*description could be given.*

*James A. Muncie (94)*

In Terry's book, he breaks down the number of sightings each year and their interesting sudden incremental increase between the years 2003 to 2013 in the United States:

*"In 2003 there were five orbs sighted and in 2004 the total was ten. In 2005 there were thirteen orbs sighted and the following year there were sixteen. In 2007, the count jumped to forty-six, followed by seventy-eight in 2008. 102 orbs were sighted in 2009 and 164 in 2010. 2011 had 305 and 2012 came in with 648. Last year, in 2013, 868 orbs were sighted over the U.S" (95)*

Terry notes that previously, prior to 2003, UFOs were hard to catch. People were looking, but it was difficult to just go out and have a UFO sighting. Since 2003 forward, there seems to be a shift in the strategy of these orange orbs. They want to be seen! The Orange Orb phenomena are not just an American phenomena but "the Orb Invasion" is happening worldwide.

What are these orbs? Terry believes that these are connected with "intelligent people". From where he doesn't know. They are here to be seen and the ultimate goal in his summation is that they are going to propel the disclosure of their existence. He believes that they are coming through a wormhole or a portal to get here. He noted that there has been, over the past couple of years, more incidents of landings increasing as well as people encountering passengers of these vehicles. (96)

People are seeing triangular-shaped craft in the vicinity of these orb sightings. Ray believes that these triangle craft are connected and almost act as the orb's home base. He also believes that the orbs are not the vehicle, but they are often seen in a triangular formation. What's interesting is that in 1967, during the month of February, between the 20th and 27th, glowing orange or red objects were reported at least five times, typically hovering at low altitude and or pacing cars. This occurred from the east coast to the mountain states. (97)

Ray thinks that they attach to the black triangle UFOs. He believes that the orange orbs are made out of a substance that wraps around a metallic ball or craft. It's a type of cloak and the color of the orbs can be changed. They have large and small crafts. These orbs, Terry believes, can hold not just one vehicle but several of them. On the *Grimerica* show, he proclaims to have a photo that he recently received with a picture of an orange orb. It looks like there are between ten to fifteen craft that are visible inside the orb when magnifying the image! (98)

He feels that the color orange is specific for a reason. The color orange is specifically chosen because of the similarity of the setting sun! He feels it is meant to be a peaceful image, one that would evoke peace. They are the "attention getter" and they want us to get "used to them" by using the orange orbs to get our attention all across the country and the world. He believes that "their message is that we are here but do not be frightened. The "disclosure" of their existence is imminent.

It's not just Terry Ray that feels that disclosure is inevitable. Dr. Steven Greer, who founded the Disclosure Project, states that when these "interstellar visitors are here, sometimes their entire craft is in the 3D or 4D world, but other times we are only seeing a hint of the craft, the energy form. We are just seeing part of them, an energy field like a sphere or a triangle, which is a trans-dimensional form. I guess we will have to wait and see if disclosure ever happens. The subject of UFOs and Bigfoot has exploded over the past several years and it seems that eventually, the levee will break. I was confident I was getting closer to discovering if the two were connected. I then started to question if they could possibly be one and the same.

# 13

# MYSTERY MAN AT MIRANDA'S PUB

One early evening a few summers ago on a Saturday, with light still in the sky, I decided to meet up with some friends at a local bar called Miranda's Pub. It was a random move. I had never been there before, but I was curious to check it out. The establishment had been on my mind, especially because it played a part in the lore of Leominster and Bigfoot. The infamous bar where the man barges in to explain that he saw a "monster" and then he suddenly disappears.

The place was a typical old-school bar with a couple of pool tables, dartboards, a few video games and a pleasant surprise, several couches scattered about. I quickly scanned the bar. As a habit, I do this all the time. I was trained to shoot when I was younger by an Army Sniper who is now a current Chief of Police in Massachusetts. He would explain to me that when he would walk into a public place, he would quickly glance around and see how many people were in the room, how many exits, and if there were any potential threats.

It all stems from his military and police training. At eighteen, it was hilarious to me at the time that he would do this. But now in the day and age in which we live, where a mother was recently randomly targeted in a grocery store and attacked with her throat slit, it seems like a good habit to have. It has started to seem necessary to be more mindful of your surroundings. I find myself doing this every time I am in a public place.

There were only about five people in the bar. An entire row of stools available. My friends and I saddled up to the bar. There were three of us. We ordered a round of beers and started to unwind. About thirty minutes or so later, I noticed this older couple come into the bar. I would say that they were in their early fifties. Their entrance into the bar had a dramatic effect. The door opening up, the light from the outside sun blinding the patrons inside for a few seconds, only the couple's silhouettes visible, until the door closed behind them.

I don't know what it was. But I was completely focused on them, especially the guy who wore tinted circle sunglasses. With those glasses, he resembled a heavy set John Lennon. He was limping with a cane. If I had to quickly sum him up, he had the look of a biker, like he could be an extra in a Hell's Angels movie. He had a seriousness about him and he looked like one tough dude.

There were still several bar stools to my left that were unoccupied. He sat down right next to me. I greeted him with a nod and received a soft "Hey man" as I continued to talk with my friends. The girl that was with him seemed very fidgety, looking around the room with a sense of subtle panic. It was odd. He seemed to be a little bit more under control but he indeed had the same vibe. It was nervous energy. For this reason, I was on "high alert".

As usual, my conversational topics were around the world of UFOs and Bigfoot and my friends who are all "ball-busters" continued to make Sasquatch jokes and the like. That's Leominster.

The mysterious man to the left of me then started to chime in after I mentioned something about UFOs. I can't recall what the exact subject was that triggered his involvement in the conversation, but he was all in. I introduced myself and he gave me his name. Not his real name, but a one-word nickname, Mouse. I thought to myself laughing, "*What the hell, did this guy just give me his name like it's a freaking codename, like Falcon and the Snowman?*" We started to discuss Ancient Astronaut Theory and then we started to dive into different books about UFOs and conspiracy theories. I was able to finish his sentences regarding authors of UFO cases, elements of UFO cases and books that we have both have read.

My friends had stopped talking and at this time they were just listening to me and Mouse going back and forth like we had been friends forever. But in the back of my mind, I was still on guard. Who the hell is this guy? The girl he was with would lean in from time to time listening to us talk and then would glance around the room again.

Then it dawned on me. I devour books and I am always going to the library and picking up books that are transferred from all over the Central Massachusetts library system. He was talking about the books that I currently had out at the time! I literally got the chills. I had three specific books that I was currently reading that he referenced and brought up! I thought that it was more than a coincidence.

It was almost as if he had looked up my account and was reading off the list of books that I had taken out of the library. He brought up the titles of the books almost one after another, and I didn't give him any clues that I picked up on it. I thought to myself. Coincidence? Synchronicity?

We then talked Bigfoot and I told him that I was one of the guys that cast the print that was in the local papers. "I thought you looked familiar!" Mouse said. Then the next words to come out of his mouth floored me. Like he was about to tell a bad joke, he looked around the room and then leaned in. He was whispering. He told me that he knows that UFOs and Bigfoots are real because he's an ex-Naval Intelligence Officer. I think I heard my heart beating out of my chest at this point. Holy Crap! He then continued "And you know what...?"

He leans in even closer to me and looks me dead in the eyes and says "You are so lucky you went to the newspaper about what you found out there in Leominster State Forest." I looked at him with a puzzled face and tried to read between the lines about what he was referring to. He spoke with such certainty and conviction with what he said next. "Bigfoot isn't an animal, it's an alien. And the powers that be would have you killed because they don't want anyone to know about it."

At this point, I was starting to sweat like I had stumbled upon some crazy secret. I think I had. I have my license to carry. I wasn't carrying on this day, but I wish I had it on me. I started to fear for my life a bit at that moment. Something wasn't right. Was this guy sent to scare the shit out of me? If he was, he was doing a great job. He then went on to explain his beliefs and said that the works of writer and researcher David Icke, even though they may seem crazy, are actually pretty much in line with the truth about all of this. "Are you serious, I mean, who would have killed us? The government?" I asked.

Mouse reached for his wallet, took out some money to pay his tab and stood up. He looked around the room again as if looking for someone in particular. His girl followed his move and got up as well. "I don't want to talk about it...here...we should meet somewhere safe like my place and then we can talk in private." I shuddered at the thought.

He grabbed a pencil and a Keno slip and wrote down his email address. Then one of my friends commented on Mouse's tattoo on his right arm. "Hey, what's that tattoo?" Mouse turned over his arm and I gasped. It was a black panther in the same position and in the same stance and on the same arm as my tattoo of a blue tiger! My friends looked at me in amazement and we both muttered "Weird". I showed Mouse my tattoo and he was in "awe" of us both having similar tattoos. My friend said, "Dude, it's like you guys are long lost brothers!" Mouse handed me the paper with his contact email. "Shoot me a note and we can set something up." I don't like to be out in public much so meeting at my place would be best." And then he left the bar.

My friends turned to me and we talked about how crazy that whole scene was. I was meant to be there to meet him. I am not afraid of anyone, but this guy scared me to death. I had no idea if I was going to walk out of this bar and have a van pull up with a bunch of guys in ski masks throwing a bag over my head, peeling out, never to be seen again. I left without any issues. I have stayed in touch with Mouse but haven't had the chance to connect with him again. I have to admit, I am a little reluctant to learn any more if my life would be in danger.

I am planning on reaching out soon so we can talk further, but I have been a little hesitant. Bigfoot is an alien. I didn't sleep that night.

# 14

# IS THERE A UFO AND BIGFOOT CONNECTION?

There are several theories about Bigfoot that are starting to take hold in the public's consciousness now, with an even stronger grip. There are standard theories that the creature, known as Sasquatch, is an undiscovered animal or a potential "missing link". The idea that Bigfoot is some kind of early human that never evolved. These theories have been discussed to no end. They will probably continue until a real Bigfoot body emerges.

Theories that these elusive creatures are a people like us, that they are human and not an animal are gaining traction. Referred to as "The Forest People" or "The Sasquatch People", this theory has been more widely accepted due to recent DNA findings. There are efforts by some like Dr. Melba Ketchum and Dr. Brian Sykes who are attempting to get real DNA evidence to not only prove that these creatures do indeed exist, but what they really are.

Due to the strangeness that comes with Sasquatch or Bigfoot, there are also other theories of what Bigfoot could be. Theories that the Sasquatch is actually an alien or an interdimensional creature has also gained in popularity. So much so, that an entire episode of *Ancient Aliens* asked the question *"Is Bigfoot Really an Alien?"*

There are several stories that point to this as a reality. What is interesting is what the researchers before me have concluded about UFOs and Bigfoot.

Both UFOs and Bigfoot seem to be in the same area. One of these areas is the "lover's lane" spots that teenagers would frequent with their significant other. In the *Bigfoot Casebook*, written by Janet and Colin Bord in 1982 (an updated version was published in 2006), the authors write about Bigfoot sightings and the UFO sightings that have occurred in those same areas. They reference a case from Kentucky in July of 1962:

*In July 1962, two young couples were in a parked car near Mount Vernon, Rockcastle County, Kentucky, when a Bigfoot hunched up on all fours hopped up to the car. They said it was covered in hair and about the size of a man, and growled at them. The number of cases in which Bigfeet take an interest in courting couples in cars suggests that this is more than chance or coincidence. Such couples parked in unfrequented "lovers' lane" areas also seem to attract more than their normal share of attention from UFOs and associated phenomena. Whether this is characteristic behavior will eventually help in solving the puzzle presented by Bigfoot and UFOs remains to be seen.* (99)

I stopped to think. What if Mouse is right? That Bigfoots are indeed aliens? After I had done a little research, I discovered that there are several stories over the years of Bigfoot seen along with UFOs that gives credence to the theory...the theory that Bigfoot is much more than we think it is...that Bigfoot is indeed an alien.

These are not "new' theories, some of these were oral

stories from years past that we were told were just Indian folklore and myth. Dr. Franklin Reuhl's article for *The Huffington Post*, entitled, *"Is Bigfoot Possibly an Alien Entity?"* contains the first story that alludes to this interconnected theory. It takes place in 1888:

> *A cattleman described an encounter with friendly Indians in Humboldt County, California. They led him to a cave where he saw a hefty humanoid creature covered in long, shiny black hair, with no neck, sitting cross-legged. One Indian told him three of these "Crazy Bears" had been cast out of a small moon that dropped from the sky and landed. The "moon" then ascended back into the air. So it's highly likely the "Crazy Bears" were really Bigfoots, and the "moon," a spacecraft. (100)*

There is another story emanating out of the state of Tennessee. The book *Evidence for Bigfoot* recalls a similar story from the 1880s where an Indian led a man to a cave in Tennessee where a hairy manlike creature was living. The Indians would provide it food on a regular basis. They believed that this creature and others like it came from the 'moons' which landed from time to time in the valley. (101)

It's a fact that there has been so much secrecy and denial around UFOs. The same can be said of Bigfoot. There have been reports of Park Rangers destroying Bigfoot tracks that were discovered in National Forests as well as blocking off normal access routes where prints were found. Reports of rangers restricting areas to hikers after Bigfoot sightings or closing trails when trackways have been discovered. One must ask themselves, why would they do that? I find it a bit curious that government employees are destroying evidence that might prove that Sasquatch is real.

There have been reports from UFO "landing areas" as well as close encounter sightings of Bigfoot where a sulfuric smell is noted, similar to the smell of rotten eggs. I find it very interesting that both of these phenomena seem to have the same smell. That leads me to believe that they are either coming from the same place or using the same method to get here. They both seem to have the ability to appear and disappear. They could both appear and disappear in the same way, which creates that undeniable stench.

Thinking further about the connection between Bigfoot and UFOs, there are definitely some similarities. People have begun to come forward with stories of interacting with Sasquatch and that they have communicated with them and have received a similar message like the ones received by UFO abductees. The message to humanity is the same, protect planet earth before we destroy it. People have reportedly communicated with aliens and Sasquatch the same way, through mental telepathy.

Ironically Ray Wallace, who was known to be the person who faked Bigfoot prints by making large wooden ones that he would strap to his feet, made some surprising claims. These Bigfoot tracks were found in Humboldt County, Northern California. It was in the same area where the Patterson / Gimlin footage was shot of the Bigfoot known as "Patty". Coincidentally, it's the same county as mentioned above in the Indian story from 1888 too!

Ray Wallace sent letters to Author and Journalist, a skeptic turned Bigfoot believer John Green. Ray claimed in his letters to Green that he had film footage of Bigfoot...over three hours of it. He told Green that he was feeding a Bigfoot apples from his truck window. He also claimed that he had spent hours being interrogated by government officials who believed that the creatures were dropped off by UFOs. "That he knew of lost gold mines that were inhabited by Bigfoots; that Bigfoot skeletons were being sold to Pentagon officials; and that he had captured two Bigfoots, only to have them escape." (102)

It is hard for people to believe these stories. They need to experience it firsthand for them to understand and believe that something is really going on out there. People are in contact with things that we still don't fully understand. As odd as the Bigfoot sightings and experiences may sound, imagine adding another layer with UFOs. A UFO (Unidentified Flying Object) doesn't have to be a spaceship or a misidentified aircraft of human origin, It can be an orb or ball of light, some kind of aerial anomaly. There are several cases over the years, across the country that involve credible witnesses with events involving both of these unexplained phenomena. Some of these witnesses even being police officers.

On July 31st, 1966, in Presque Island State Park, Pennsylvania, four adults, two couples and two young children are visiting from New York. They are checking out Beach 6 when their vehicle gets stuck in the sand. They all try to push it out but to no avail. One of the male adults is given a ride to go and retrieve a tow truck. Minutes later police officers arrive and promise to come back in a little while and will help if they still need it.

As the five of them, the other male, the two women, the two young children are waiting in the car for the tow-truck, they notice a star-like object that gets brighter and dim and then starts to move across the sky. Then it comes straight down, hovers and then seems to land in the woods nearby. The UFO causes the car to vibrate. When the police arrive, the carload explains what they saw in the sky. The police officers take them seriously and then the officers take the last remaining male adult with them into the woods. He wanted to show the officers the vicinity where the UFO seems to have landed.

While the girls and the kids are left alone in the stranded car waiting for them to return, they witness a six foot, ape looking humanoid walking towards them. It emerges from the same area that the police had entered to locate the landed craft. The creature circles the vehicle, even clawing at the car, leaving marks. This scene caused one of the women to scream. The creature then walked back into the woods, The UFO then coincidentally shoots back up into the sky. The police returned to find the women in a state of shock. The Pennsylvania State Police and the Air Force arrive to investigate. The case was included in Project Blue Book #10798 and was classified as being "unsolved". (103)

Stan Gordon is the author of *Silent Invasion: The Pennsylvania UFO-Bigfoot Casebook* that discusses the Bigfoot sightings that occurred over several days in 1973, in various distant places throughout the state of Pennsylvania. There were daylight sightings of a Bigfoot creature and other sightings with more than one. There were also reports of UFOS and Bigfoots seen together.

Something to note, acclaimed UFO author and researcher Raymond E. Fowler received a phone call asking if he also investigated not just UFO reports and sightings but if he handled Bigfoot reports as well? He replied to the caller, "Well, I do now." Astonishingly, it was the Massachusetts State Police who had reached out to Fowler. They were starting to receive Bigfoot reports on top of the reported sightings of UFOs in Massachusetts!

Stan Gordon, in 1970, started a research group called the Westmoreland County UFO Study Group (WCUFOSG). Among the volunteers that made up the research group were scientists, engineers, technicians, as well as retired military specialists, who could provide an open-minded investigation into the cases reported.

There were UFO and Bigfoot reports occurring in Pennsylvania that were frequently being referred to WCUFOSG to investigate. These reports originated from law enforcement agencies and the news media. The team was able to discern the hoaxes and the cases that seemed to be misidentifications. But the ones that were unexplained and involved the weird aspect of Bigfoot seemed to change people's minds about what they were actually dealing with.

In an interview with the *Examiner.com*, Stan Gordon talks about the connection of the UFO and Bigfoot phenomena:

*First of all let me say that if I had not been directly involved in the investigation of these cases as they were being reported, I would be very skeptical of the reality of such incidents. When I first began in my early years of research into UFOs and Bigfoot encounters, I never gave any consideration that the two phenomena might somehow be related. Listening first hand to the accounts from frightened witnesses sometimes just minutes after their encounters, and finding bits and pieces of evidence at the scene of the events was very convincing.*

*The eyewitness reports of strange lights or aerial phenomena accompanying the appearance in the same area of a Bigfoot creature from such widespread areas could not be ignored. Let me stress again, most UFO incidents do not involve a Bigfoot creature, and most Bigfoot cases do not have a UFO observation associated*

167

*with it. Most witnesses that we interviewed had no prior interest in such unusual matters. In some cases, those involved asked us why the strange lights and the creatures seemed to show up at about the same time.*

*There is a small percentage of cases however where observers have seen both a UFO and Bigfoot at the same time and location. From the reports I have received from across the country and around the world, such cases might be much more common, but many researchers have been reluctant to publish such accounts for fear of ridicule from their peers. I don't know if any direct connection exists between UFOs and Bigfoot, but it is my position not to pretend that such cases do not exist, but to try to find some answers and to encourage others to share such accounts. (104)*

In 1973, in Fayette County, Pennsylvania, a red UFO was seen by fifteen people. It slowly made its way down from the sky and seemed to land in a pasture. There were a few brave souls in the group. There were three young boys, armed with guns, who decided to go out and investigate. They came upon the pasture where the glowing UFO had landed. The craft was reportedly a hundred feet wide and had now changed its color to white.

They heard a cry coming from near the object and then there was a terrible smell. The three men looked over to see several 7-8 foot hairy creatures walking upright along the fence line and heading in their direction. One of the boys raised his gun and fired a tracer over one of the Bigfoot's head. The Bigfoot raised his hand in the air and in that instant, the UFO vanished. The boys fired more shots at the Bigfoot who simply walked away, unaffected. A state trooper inspected the scene and found a "circle of earth glowing so brightly it outshone his flashlight." (105)

Then there is the case in 1973 where an anonymous phone call was received at the Westmoreland UFO Center in Pennsylvania, run by investigator Stan Gordon. The caller explained that three women, while driving, reportedly watched a UFO land and then amazingly the hatch door opens and several seven-foot-tall hairy creatures come out of the landed craft and run into the woods.

Per the Huffington Post article by Dr. Reuhl, there were also several intriguing UFO sightings around British Columbia during the summer of 1976:

*"In August of 1976, after a series of UFO sightings around Rutland, British Columbia, Canada, several men and their children saw a hairy ape-like entity, six to seven feet tall roaming about a mountainside. They also found a clump of hair that was sent to the Royal Canadian Mounted Police for identification. Laboratory analysis confirmed it was primate hair, but, significantly, it could not be matched to any known species on earth!"* (106)

Years earlier in 1968, legendary writer of the strange, Brad Steiger, who has written and co-written over 183 books regarding the mysteries of the universe, thought that there might be a connection with UFOs and Bigfoot. Due to the amassing amount of reports of UFOs and Bigfoot seen together or in the same area, he decided to write an article connecting the phenomena.

Steiger was living in northeastern Iowa. In a town which is snuggled in a valley surrounded by a wooded area. During the mid-1960s, the residents would be driving along the roads at night and then they started seeing UFOs in the sky. Then, they began to see large shadowy creatures in the ditches close to the road. Due to a number of caves in the area, the residents started to question whether there were monsters living within them.

A local police officer named Jim approached Steiger and told him that he had received a lot of reports of close encounters that he deemed credible. He also stated that he himself had witnessed these UFOs flying low while he was on patrol. Steiger then got an idea to form a group that would research the UFO and Bigfoot phenomena. The group consisted of retired Army and Marine veterans as well as police officers. The group's goal was to establish whether or not the lumbering forest giants existed and to discern whether or not the creatures had a clear connection to the UFO phenomena.

Brad Steiger talks about how one of these Bigfoot creatures just disappeared out of thin air:

*In July 1972, the Missouri Monster, "MoMo," was terrifying the good folks of Louisiana, Missouri, and gaining national and international notice and our team was all over the case...along with dozens of heavily armed men with their own motives for capturing or shooting the Bigfoot that had raised so much ruckus. On July 19th, MoMo was surrounded in a patch off Marzolf Hill by a "posse" of at least 25 men who had no intentions of allowing the creature to get away. Their intentions were to bring MoMo in, alive or dead. And then MoMo was just gone. Vanished. Without a trace.*

*Regardless of how many men combed the patch that they had surrounded on Marzolf Hill, the mysterious Bigfoot had vanished...Although our own Bigfoot/UFO investigative team continued to keep track of cases suggestive of the involvement of such unknown creatures and in the immediate area of the sightings of unidentified aerial vehicles, investigation after investigation produced similar results: the gigantic creature simply vanished.* (107)

There was a case involving triangular UFOS and Bigfoot being seen together in Arkansas in 1996. A witness and several friends were walking through the woods near the witnesses home when they saw a bright light which got their attention. Then they saw what looked like Bigfoot creatures standing near three triangular craft, the craft stood hovering in the woods, with beams of light emanating from its three corners. It was reported that it looked like the Bigfoots were the pilots of the craft. That theory was proven correct when the creatures smelled the air as if they were aware of the witnesses' presence. The creatures entered their craft and took off in a blinding flash of light which knocked the witnesses to the ground. (108)

In an article by Micah Hanks, for *Mysterious Universe,* entitled: *"Curious Cryptohominids: A link between Aliens and Bigfoot?"* Hanks brings to light the fact that there have been some serious studies performed in trying to solve the riddle of the connection between the two phenomena.

*"But all the more bizarre speculation put aside, there have actually been studies performed in the past that sought to try and explain why there are, in fact, trends between Bigfoot and UFO sightings. Peter Leeson, a BB&T Professor for the Study of Capitalism at George Mason University, undertook a similar task in 2008. Leeson, who admitted having an interest in UFOs in an economics blog, began plotting UFO sightings on a chart that similarly placed states where Bigfoot sightings occurred graphically. Even in the early stages, Leeson described "an intriguing pattern," in which he found that states that had more UFO sightings also appeared to be having more Bigfoot sightings. Guest blogging for the New York Times, Leeson wrote*

that "six of the top ten U.F.O. and Bigfoot states are the same: Washington, Oregon, New Mexico, Alaska, Wyoming, and Colorado. Two states, Washington and Oregon, are among both categories' top five." (109)

# 15

# BIGFOOT AND THE ORANGE ORBS

There has been some kind of weird connection with colored balls of light and Bigfoot. Some of these lights are blue and a lot of them are orange. I spoke with Mark Parra, a Bigfoot researcher from Colorado, who has encountered the blue orbs of light at his research area. These balls of light, or orbs as many have called them, are seen in areas where there have been Bigfoot sightings.

During a night investigation in Leominster State Forest, via the Granite Street entrance, a friend and I experienced the orange orb phenomena together. This time, it almost seemed to respond to my friend's statements and the exact place where he was pointing! My friend, as well as his wife, have seen a huge orange fireball, with a tail, almost like sparks, fly over their house on several occasions towards the swamp behind their property. They have both had multiple sightings from inside as well as outside the house. This is the same area that the two orange orbs I witnessed were traveling towards. This is also in the vicinity where several boys saw a tall dark figure walking away from them.

So we decided on an impromptu night trip into Leominster

State Forest. I had the sense that we would be seeing something, but not what we were hoping for. You want to walk back into those woods and have a Bigfoot encounter. You want something to happen to you that would tell you that they do exist and that the footprints you found are not from some normal human being. I had the inclination that we would see something when we went out there. But it would be something in the sky, not on the ground. I was hoping to see another orange orb. Well, we did.

We started walking towards the trail where the Bigfoot tracks were found and we maybe got about a half mile into the forest when we both felt like we were being watched. It was that spooky feeling again. We had insufficient flashlights for the trek but we were hoping that the moonlight would give us enough light once our eyes had adjusted. We weren't sure if we were hearing branches and twigs breaking but it sounded like something big was in the darkness close by. We both looked at our feeble lighting we held in our hands and admitted we should walk back to the car and retrieve something stronger.

It was January so we knew that there shouldn't be any black bears out as they would be hibernating around this time. We got back to the car and felt a bit more comfortable at the parking area. My friend searched his car for another flashlight and turned up empty. We were chatting and he looked over at the faint silhouette of Bobcat Mountain in the distance. He raised his arm and pointed in the direction of the peak of Bobcat and said out loud that "we need to get out to that point right there. No one goes out all the way. I bet we would find something Bigfoot related right there!"

And almost as if on cue a few minutes later, as we were continuing to talk, out of the left of our peripheral vision, a reddish-orange orb, the size of a basketball appeared to materialize out of thin air. I grabbed my friend by the arm and said, "Do you see what I am seeing?" "Yes, an orange orb moving in the direction of Bobcat Mountain!" came his excited reply. "Are you fucking kidding me? What the hell is it?" I said. My friend said, "It's probably a Bigfoot coming into the forest to eat!" We both, even though we should have, didn't laugh at this crazy statement.

The orb, glowing orange and most definitely self-luminescent, finally came into contact with the edge of the woods leading to Bobcat Mountain. It moved in the same fashion as the ones that I had seen before. Slow, consistent and silent. But it was alone. Once it hit the outline of the trees, it started to move through the woods, it lit up all the trees and everything around it in a widened circle. The forest in the immediate area was illuminated by it. We knew it wasn't a figment of our imagination. We were both seeing something real. It was now maneuvering through the trees! It was an amazing sight to see and not once did we feel compelled to pull out our phones to take a picture! We were almost in a trance-like state.

The orb literally came right to the spot where my friend had pointed and then all of a sudden hovered over the area for a second and then shot straight down into the ground. The same spot that he was pointing to just moments ago! The light went off. All you could hear was complete silence, then I was aware of the sound of heavy breathing. Both my friend and I didn't say a word. We were out of breath as if we just got back from a run. The forest was quiet aside from our heavy breathing. It took a few seconds for us to snap out of it. We were almost in a state of shock staring at the spot where the orb had plummeted straight down.

All I could think about was something coming out of that

orange thing and heading our way. An alien or a Bigfoot-like creature. I laughed at the thought, but it was a nervous one because it felt like the scene out of a bad horror movie. It was a moment that will forever be burned into my mind. I believe I may have been the first one to suggest we get out of there. "I am waiting for something to come cruising up the hill towards us and I don't have a great feeling about this! This is crazy!" I shouted out loud, finally revealing my thoughts verbally. My friend agreed.

I assumed he was expecting the same thing. He didn't say a word. We climbed back into his truck and got out of there. We kept glancing behind us to see if anything was following us out. I didn't like the fact that I had the feeling we would see this orange orb and then it appeared! It appeared in the spot that my friend had been talking about...where we will be sure to find some evidence of Bigfoot.

"What are they doing listening? Are they reading our minds now?!" I asked. "And who the hell are they?" my friend responded. This was on a Tuesday. I remember that later on, I had remarked at the weird consistency of seeing something or having something happen to me on Tuesdays. My first orange orb sighting, and now this one. What the hell!?

Little would I know, that just days later, I would read about the theory of author and researcher, John A. Keel, who wrote *The Mothman Prophecies.* He believed that UFOS were linked with the paranormal and the supernatural phenomena that have been taking place throughout our known history. The timeframe of Keel's UFO research was during the sixties. He also believed that the phenomena would appear on a particular day and time frame. Based on his data mining of all the UFO sightings, he discovered that a majority of the sightings appeared all over the country every Wednesday between the hours of 8:30 PM and 10:30 PM! They had a freaking schedule?!

These balls of light have been reported recently by many Bigfoot researchers. Some of these researchers are starting to believe that there is some sort of connection. (110) The following day after the night of the "Ghost Box" incident revealed this very fact. One of the individuals we were reviewing the ghost hunting equipment with had slept over.

He woke up early the following morning and stepped outside the front door around 4:30-5:00 AM. Floating in the sky above the road directly across the street near the street lamp was a basketball-sized orange orb! It hovered and floated for a few seconds in full view of him before it quickly took off and went straight up into the air! The witness revealed this to me while we were out in the woods that night after I described my orange orb encounter in Leominster State Forest. The witness didn't tell anyone about his experience until after hearing my story!

These orange orbs have also been seen indoors. My wife Amy, when we first bought our home, recalled waking up in the middle of the night and noticing this orange/bronze ball of light, the size of a golf ball, flying around in our house! I was sound asleep and she couldn't wake me up. I wish she was able to. She didn't tell me this until years later. It reminded me of Betty Andreasson's encounter in 1944 in Leominster when this small ball of light had affixed itself to her forehead.

This also reminded me of a similar experience as a child. I was very young, between six and seven years old. It happened a few times to me. In the middle of the night, I had a sense of fear as if something was in the room. The room would be dark, except for a light coming from a small nightlight plugged into the wall.

From my peripheral vision, I would see what I could only describe as a small ball of fire floating off to my right at eye level. I would estimate it to be the size of a golf ball. I thought that I must have been dreaming. But it seemed as if it was real, due to the fact that this ball of light was bright enough to cause me to squint my right eye! When I would look to the right to see what it was, there would be nothing there. It would disappear. I would look straight ahead and it would slowly come back to its original position. It scared me so much. But after time, the memories just got tucked away.

What do the Native Americans believe when it comes to these lights? There are Native American cultures that associate these lights with Bigfoot! What's interesting to note is that certain Native American shamans are said to have the ability to shape-shift in order to travel long distances. They can purportedly shapeshift into different animals and even transform into a pure sphere of light, as big as a common basketball, pulsating as if it were breathing. Many also believe that these balls of light, which are commonly seen near Native American locations of significance and history, are the spirits of Native Americans that have passed away.

The Marfa lights of Texas are balls of light that have been seen and known of by the Apache people in that region for over 100 years. They were perceived to be spirits. According to settlers during the late 19th century, the lights were the ghosts of massacred Indians. Later on, in the early twentieth century, Texans believed that the lights were spirits guarding hidden treasure." (111)

In the book *Bigfoot*, the co-authors Riggs and Burnette discuss how mysterious lights seem to be synonymous with Bigfoot sightings,

*"The animals are, indeed, frequently seen immediately after the appearance of mysterious lights, and as has been shown, they are definitely sometimes associated with equally mysterious lights and has been shown, they are definitely sometimes associated with equally mysterious blackouts and power outages, especially of vehicles. What confuses the issue is similar light and energy phenomena are also frequently associated with paranormal phenomena, such as classic haunting cases."* (112)

*"Not only are there long-term established histories of Bigfoot-type creature sightings near the Big Thicket and Brown Mountain Ghost Light locations, but a brief survey of the available literature will show the Yakima Indian Reservation Lights in Washington, The Gonzales Lights in Louisiana, The Gordon Light in Arkansas, and the Hornet Spook Light location in Missouri, also have histories of numerous and repeated sightings of mysterious hairy primates nearby where the lights occur."* (113)

They are not the only authors who have noticed this connection of Bigfoot with the strange balls of light. Lisa A. Shiel, the author of *Forbidden Bigfoot* believes that there is something going on between Bigfoot and these orbs. Lisa states that *"Sightings involving glowing orbs and Bigfoot, though rare, do exist in the annals of paranormal research. The synchronicity of Bigfoot and glowing orbs when they appear in the same area but not at the same time seems even more prevalent than sightings of the two together."* (114)

Sali Sheppard-Wolford wrote a book entitled *Valley of the Skookum*. She writes about her years living in the remote wilderness with her children and her youngest daughter, Autumn Williams, where they had encountered Bigfoot, UFOs, and basketball sized orange orbs. There are Native American

179

cultures that believe that Sasquatch is half spirit and that these balls of light, the orange orbs, are Bigfoot themselves.

Khat Hansen, a Choctaw Medicine woman, told the authors of the book *Bigfoot*, Tom Burnette and Rob Riggs that, *"Some of the cases of these ghosts lights are the intermediary phase of Bigfoot moving from the spirit world to this reality or vice versa. Native American traditions of the Choctaw and Yaqui, for example, claim there are Shamans who have developed the power to transform themselves into a ball of light."*

Author Rob Riggs' research also uncovered, just like the Native American shamans abilities to shapeshift into balls of light, that the same is rumored to be true among the Cajuns in South Louisiana of voodoo practitioners who can shapeshift into the Rougarou, a Bigfoot-type hairy creature, and the fifolat, a bright ball of light. (115)

In southern California, another Native American tribe believes in a similar creature and their connection with the orbs or lights that are often seen with Sasquatch sightings or experiences:

> *"The Gabrielino Indians of southern California believed in the existence of Towis or Takwis, a giant hairy cannibal, who was also associated with bright flashes of light and flying luminescent balls. This lore dates back to 200 years." (116)*

There are several stories from around the country that I have found that include these mysterious orbs being seen in the vicinity of Bigfoot encounters. In the book *Bigfoot Casebook*, the author talks about the following case:

> *Early in October 1973, near Galveston, Indiana, Jeff Martin or Jim Mays (we have two reports of this case with two*

different names, one of them presumably being a pseudonym, but we do not know which) was fishing one evening. He looked over his shoulder to see an ape-like figure watching him in the dusk from about 20 feet away. He called to it but it slipped off into the twilight. A short while later he felt a touch on his shoulder and behind him stood the creature, a sandy-colored Bigfoot. It ran swiftly away and Jeff/Jim followed behind. As it crossed a road he could see its feet flapping on the hard surface.

Then it leaped into a ditch and vanished into the trees.

Almost instantaneously a glowing bronze light rose from the woods and shot away in the sky. Two days later Jeff/Jim returned with their fiancé, her father, and two friends. As they drove to the area they were followed by an aerial light that disappeared before the journey's end. At the place where Jeff/Jim had last seen the creature, it was standing amid tall weeds. One of the parties thought that when they turned their beams on it the beams seemed weaker.

Using the surrounding herbage as a guide, they estimated its height as between 8 or 9 feet, and although two of the party had retreated to the car in fear, the others shouted questions and curses at it. As it failed to respond in any way, they tried throwing rocks, but they could not see whether the missiles bounced off, missed, or went through the creature.

Whatever their aim, the creature did not move. Because of another car on the track, they had to move their own car, and when they returned the Bigfoot could no longer be seen. Of possible significance, in this case, is the fact that Jeff/Jim's fiance's father had since 1965 had a dozen or so UFO sightings, and on one occasion had exchanged flashed *signals with a UFO. (117)*

Orbs played a part on the Bigfoot stage in Pennsylvania. And yet another encounter, in Westmoreland County, the same county which had a UFO, shaped like a bell, crash in the town of Kecksburg back in 1965, has had its healthy share of Bigfoot sightings.

On September 27th in 1973, two girls witnessed a 7-8 foot, *white* Bigfoot watching them while they were playing outside. The eyes of the Bigfoot were glowing red and it stood watching the girls behind some trees nearby. If that wasn't enough, the girls stated that the Bigfoot was holding *a glowing orb* in its hand. They ran home to tell their father, who went out looking for what they saw and came back an hour later telling everyone to stay out of the woods. One wonders what the father might have actually witnessed in those woods for him to be so adamant that the girls stay inside the house. (118)

With shows like *Finding Bigfoot* and *Mountain Monsters*, there are more and more Bigfoot hunters/researchers out there joining in the hunt for the elusive animal. But are we really sure we are dealing with an animal? And if they are not, and they are something else, like an alien, how are they getting here? Are they already living here? Are they coming from another dimension like some researchers propose? And if they are traveling in between dimensions, how are they doing this? Could the orbs of light be the answer to this question?

So let's say for the sake of argument that this is the truth, that Sasquatch is an interdimensional creature. The feat of traveling from dimension to dimension sounds like it would be quite sophisticated. In order to have this ability to travel between dimensions, it would seem to me that a simple animal could not do this. This sounds like a highly evolved and exceptional being. So in order to travel to other dimensions, one would think that maybe they would they need to transform themselves, into something else, like a ball of light? Can matter be turned into light? In theory, yes it can, some scientists seem to think that this is indeed a possibility.

Physicists are showing in theory, how matter can be converted into light with the use of high-powered lasers and other equipment. This is done on the quantum or subatomic level. In May of 2014, there was an article written by Ian Sample, the science correspondent for *The Guardian*. The article discussed how particle physics researchers have worked out how to make matter from pure light and are drawing up plans to demonstrate the feat within the next year. "We have shown in principle how you can make matter from light", says Steven Rose, a physicist at Imperial College in London, England.

In 1934, physicists Gregory Breit and John Wheeler first came up with this idea. "They worked out that very rarely, two particles of light, or photons, could combine to produce and electron, and its anti-matter equivalent, a positron. Electrons are particles of matter that form the outer shells of atoms in the everyday objects around us. This is done through a process called Quantum Electro Dynamics or (QED) and it shows that light and matter are interchangeable. Per Rose, they would be taking light and turning it into matter and that light and matter are interchangeable. (119)

So now we are on the cusp of learning more about how light and matter are of the same substance. Basically, think of the TV show *Star Trek* when Captain Kirk and Spock would stand together and dematerialize into light particles beam down from the ship and appear on an alien planet. Sasquatch could be doing something similar to this, converting matter into light and back again. Some long-time researchers believe that they are traveling within the orbs, essentially becoming the balls of light that people will see before or after a Bigfoot sighting or experience.

Canadian Bigfoot researcher Mike Paterson told me when out at the cottage doing research at night, he witnessed a gray smokey-like haze appear in front of him right before he felt a hairy hand touch his face! Rob Riggs speculates along these very same lines in his book that, *"Perhaps Bigfoot can actually transform his body from matter into a cloud-like vapor that becomes energy and light and then re-materializes at will..."* (120)

Khat Hansen, who I referenced earlier, a Native American, and a Choctaw Medicine woman who lives near the Nevada Mountain range, has been having encounters with Bigfoot since the age of five. She has been taught from an early age that she must respect all beings and there are ones that come here.

During an online interview, Khat Hansen discusses this belief in Bigfoot being more than just an animal in more detail,

*"Bigfoots are a spirit being who can assume a flesh and blood body. Which simply means: He is a being, a creature that has access to this world. He comes and goes off his pleasing. This is why sometimes people say they have found footprints coming from UNDER a small rock and disappearing into a small scrub brush with nothing surrounding it or just stopping in the dirt and not continuing anywhere. He can shift and leave this realm and this world when he wants. He is not limited to being here as are we. He has different gifts that he uses. That we humans have not learned or been given."* (121)

One of these gifts of the Bigfoot that Khat Hansen mentions may indeed be the ability to turn into a ball of light. People have also reported seeing balls of light when dealing with ghosts and the paranormal. Many believe that we pass on when we leave this earth and go somewhere else. That "somewhere else" could very well be another dimension. If they are a spirit being, and orbs have been seen around when ghosts or spirits are present, than this may be what people are potentially seeing.

As an example of what an orb looks like, here's an amazingly clear photo of an orb from Leominster. It has never been shared before and it was recently photographed. I was given permission to use this photo for the book. Leominster, known for its UFO history, is also known for its ghost encounters as well. The city has been featured on all the major Ghost Hunting TV series, like TAPS, Ghost Adventures, and Paranormal State. The photographer has asked to remain anonymous. She felt compelled to take out her camera as she was watching her granddaughter playing and had the impression that her husband, who had recently passed away, was there with them at the time.

She retrieved her camera and took only one picture, the one above. You will notice the perfect white ball of light and what almost seems like a train track, seeing where the orb is coming from, a light trail, but also where it is going as we can see the path ahead of the light! Or maybe the light moved in front of the lens and then went too far and came back into the frame of the shot so that it could be captured on the photo.

One of the many gifts that the Sasquatch are said to have, which Khat Hansen has alluded to, is their wisdom on how to use energy from these "high energy" areas. This energy seems to have an effect on consciousness at some levels. People have claimed to feel "zapped" during a Bigfoot encounter or experience and are soaked with the overwhelming feeling of being out of wits, crippled with disorientation and extreme fear. They almost feel like they got their brains scrambled a bit. This happened with the hikers in Leominster State Forerst. They felt like they were lost when they knew the area so well. They were overwhelmed with fear. "High Energy" areas. These "high energy" areas could be in places like October Mountain, The Bridgewater Triangle...and Leominster State Forest.

Burnette and Riggs propose that Bigfoot could be a race of beings that has a profound wisdom of this subtle energy and its relationship to consciousness and perception. They seem to be able to use this knowledge in some form of mind control or hypnosis that not only keeps them hidden from view of mankind but possibly could allow them to alter the form of themselves with these places that contain the ghost lights or balls of light, apparently in "high energy" locations.

An example of one of these high energy locations or sacred places is in the Catskills where there have been several sightings of Bigfoot as of late. In Phil Imbrogno's book *Interdimensional Universe*, the author explains how Henry Hudson who, on September 11th, 1609, sailed the Half Moon into the mouth of a great river – later named after him – during one of his many stops, a medicine man warned Hudson to stay out of the hills at night because it was the home of many earth spirits that were able to take the form of men or beasts. Spirits of the mountains were known to use magic to take people away or fall asleep for a long time. (122)

With the abundance of UFO, Bigfoot and Orb sightings, could Leominster possibly fall into one of these "high energy" places? While shooting for the show FINDING BIGFOOT in Leominster State Forest, one of the witnesses had finished shooting their film sequences and had some down time during some of the other scenes that we were shooting. The witness was hanging with the crew members and got into a discussion about what Bigfoot. They were shocked to hear what one of the crew members believed Bigfoot to be. He believed that Bigfoot is an interdimensional being that comes through portals. The witness's jaw dropped. When I initially heard this theory, I laughed at the concept. Now I am starting to think that it all makes sense.

# 16

# INTERDIMENSIONAL BIGFOOT?

Some researchers have proposed this theory that Bigfoot is indeed an alien, but one that comes here through another dimension. A dimension which from time to time will interface with our own universe. Due to the "high strangeness" associated with Bigfoot, some researchers are starting to believe that Sasquatch is both physical and nonphysical and that they live in a quantum reality. There are Native American tribes that have said all along that this is a half-animal, half-spirit. That the Bigfoot live on the border of two worlds.

Almost every single Native American tribe in North America has a name or legend regarding Sasquatch. One of them is the Hoopa Native American Tribe. Residing in the Hoopa Valley in Northern California, their reservation is in the town called Takimildin. Interestingly it is near the location of the infamous Patterson/Gimlin film, which is still today one of the best pieces of visual evidence. The film shows a Bigfoot, looking back and then walking away along Bluff Creek in 1967.

The Hoopa Indians believe that Sasquatch does indeed exist and that they live in the trees. They also strongly believe that they should be left alone. Maybe that's why people are having a hard time seeing them? If they are not invisible, then maybe they are in the trees while we are looking down on the ground for sign!

The Hoopa people also believe that Sasquatch is a creature that lives in the middle zone between both dimensions, traveling between them. Maybe this is why non-Native Americans have a hard time accepting this belief. It sounds like science-fiction. Their belief of the inter-dimensional ability of the Sasquatch was uncovered when author and researcher David Paulides, who was a former police investigator. He is an author and known for his books entitled *Missing: 411* about the various disappearances and deaths of people entering our National State Parks and Forests. David was privy to this knowledge when talking with two Hoopa Tribal police officers on the reservation while researching for his book *The Hoopa Project*.

With all of the "high-strangeness" that comes with Bigfoot, more and more researchers are leaning on this theory. Phil Imbrogno states in his last book, *Files from the Edge*, and explains his belief that *"Bigfoot and other similar monster-like entities come from a parallel reality very close to our own. These strange and often scary creatures seem to selectively interact with our world and disappear. How or why they do this is unknown, but it would explain their phantasmic nature."* (123)

In the article *Sasquatch and the Seatco Indians* by Ted Heisteman for *Disinformation.com*, the author states that the Indian tribes of the Pacific Northwest recognized Sasquatch as another local Indian tribe known as the Seatco. They were also known as "The Stick Indians."

They were described to the white settlers by the Native

Americans as being seven and a half to eight feet tall and covered with hair. They live in underground caves and have no use for tools. They are able to hunt deer by the use of hypnotism and can elude enemies through ventriloquism. The Seatco also possess a powerful medicine that renders them *invisible*. They are fond of practical jokes and often steal salmon and occasionally women. Some of the Indian tribes have intermarried with them and have Seatco blood running through their veins." (124)

What backs up this claim of invisibility is that there are several stories of Sasquatch disappearing in front of people's eyes. A group of hikers who returned from a long hike watched a nine to ten foot Sasquatch walk out onto the path and then dematerialize in front of their eyes. It completely disappeared. One of the witnesses would not leave her house for two weeks due to the fear of what she experienced. (125)

People are experiencing what some Bigfoot researchers call "Mind Speak" coming from the Bigfoot. Communicating through telepathy, like so many UFO abductee and experiencers have encountered with aliens. Witnesses describe seeing lights in the sky and then there is a Bigfoot sighting by that same witness. Or like I discussed earlier, there is the scenario where UFOs and Bigfoots are seen in the same area around the same timeframe.

Invisibility would explain how these entities can just disappear "into thin air" and become so elusive that they evade capture. Trying to comprehend these scenarios makes your head hurt. It defies the laws of physics.

Some Bigfoot have disappeared in front of someone's eyes within a flash of light. There was a case in 1974 in Pennsylvania where a woman thought she heard the local dogs making a racket outside her front door. She grabbed her 16-gauge shotgun and swung open the door only to find a seven-foot-tall Bigfoot standing in front of her. She pulled the trigger and it put its arms up and with a bright flash, it disappeared!

With every story you might hear or read about, you must keep an open mind, but then also be skeptical. There was some Bigfoot activity, which allegedly was classified by the military, on and around Edward's Air Force base in the Palmdale-Lancaster area of the Mojave Desert in California during the 1970s. These reports actually came from military personnel who were on the base.

Anonymously, various personnel reported this and stated that they were told not to fire upon the creatures, but to just observe them. With the use of Starlight scopes, the military personnel watched these Bigfoot walk through the base at night. The Bigfoots made their appearance for several days. Sometimes for several nights in a row. Then they would suddenly disappear.

They were recorded on surveillance systems and were seen inside the deep tunnel systems that are supposed to exist underneath the base. The personnel stated that the reason that these animals were not reported to the public, is because the Government could not explain what these creatures were or how they got on the base with such high security. (126)

Kewaunee Lasperitis is a researcher who claims to have communicated with the Sasquatch. They are not an animal he says, but they are a "people". He believes that there are numerous clans of Sasquatch throughout North America. He also believes that they have selected him to tell the world about their presence with his two books entitled *The Psychic Sasquatch* and *The Sasquatch People.* Many of these

Sasquatches have been working with the "Star People" claiming that they are trying to help prevent humans from destroying the earth which would negatively affect the solar system and other dimensions.

Kewaunee believes that the Sasquatch and the Star People are one in the same and that they really have two goals. First, that they protect the planet from being environmentally destroyed. This statement has been echoed since the first UFO contactees emerged. And secondly, that they find Earth people who are evolved enough to work with them. (127)

As of November 2015, he has documented over 187 cases of people's interactions with The Forest People and their interdimensional connection. Per Kewaunee, the four kinds of Sasquatch that he is aware of are the Sasquatch, the Ancient Ones, the Dog-faced looking Sasquatch and the Skunk Ape. The ancient ones have a more human-like face and round heads and the Sasquatch are more ape-like with conical heads. They are both watchers of the earth. They possess their own separate languages but prefer mental telepathy. Some can even read and write at a limited level.

And they all have names, like humans. This was told to the Indians long ago. Per Kewaunee, they are actually advanced races who see no purpose or use for technology. He also states that "They have told me and others that they were deposited here eons ago by friendly alien beings from another world. In reality, they are terrestrial extraterrestrials" (125) Kewaunee has also claimed to have been informed by an ancient one that there are "seven distinct races of their people worldwide, each at different levels of development - the yeti are the least evolved" (128)

In Janet and Colin Bord's book *The Evidence for Bigfoot and other Man-Beasts*, the authors recount several cases involving both UFOs and Bigfoot. This one, in particular, occurred in western Pennsylvania where the witness said that the Bigfoot communicated with him via mental telepathy:

*In the majority of cases, the UFOs seen by Bigfoot witnesses are lights rather than craft, as the following data will show. UFOs were reported in Pennsylvania and at Sykesville, Maryland, in 1973 in the areas where apparently non-physical Bigfeet were seen, and the Roachdale Bigfoot of 1972 is said to have appeared only hours after a mysterious glowing object had exploded silently over a field.*

*More recently, Bigfoot sightings in western Pennsylvania have apparently involved both non-physical features and UFOs. In the spring of 1979, Sam and Ruth Frew saw a large object tumbling from the sky, and two weeks afterward started hearing a strange noise, which Mrs. Frew described as follows: "The sound is not a bark, squeal, squawk, or howling sound. In fact, we don't know how to describe it. It travels quite fast. It seems like it's on one hillside one second, the next second, it's on another hill. Once anyone hears it they never forget it. It makes your skin want to crawl.'*

*Over the next three years, 'Mystery', as the family christened the strange events, revealed itself in various ways: strange smells, three-toed footprints, a continuation of the strange noises which made their farm animals nervous and mystery lights which caused bad headaches. On August 12th, 1981, Sam Frew saw a 12-foot hairy creature in the woods after receiving a mental message to 'Come back down to the gas line', which was where he saw the creature.*

*Next day he found three-toed footprints there. In July 1981, two neighbors had seen a black panther while they were driving on a country back road. They stopped very close to it and as it stood there for ten minutes they noted its four-foot-long body, equally long tail, sleek fur, small head, small pointed ears, and long legs. Finally, the animal walked slowly out of sight.*

*Later in the summer, other sightings of the black cat were reported, as were sightings of mystery lights, and of Bigfoot. Sam Frew felt that the creature had tried to communicate. It is not from this dimension; this is why you can only find a few footprints and they disappear. (129)*

Telepathy is claimed to be the primary method of communication used by Sasquatch. In the introduction from Kewaunee Lasperitis's book: *The Sasquatch People,* he explains how he got involved in this research:

*I unexpectedly became a contactee in 1979 when both a Sasquatch and ET telepathically spoke to me. It was a very startling experience but has been an ongoing process ever since. Because of my scientific background, I struggled for two years with the psychic aspect of this phenomenon until I finally stopped my denial and accepted the new reality.*

*I have now been conducting Sasquatch research for 55 years. My struggle with a resulting spiritual transformation has been sorely misunderstood by the community of researchers who believe that procuring a dead body, bones or clear photographic evidence is what this phenomenon is about. But there are no monsters here for the taking!...Despite the adolescent attitude of some scientists toward the unknown, especially involving psi, UFOs, and other elusive phenomena, many sagacious scientists realize that quantum physics and psychic phenomena are synonymous-perhaps born of the same crucible. (130)*

Many have claimed that Bigfoot have the ability to follow someone home inter-dimensionally and leave gifts for people. This has been reported by several people including Mike Paterson who we will talk with in the next chapter as I had the opportunity to interview him for this book. This is yet another aspect of Sasquatch and the supernatural.

This invisibility piece seems to be an essential skill for hunting game. A hunter and his son decided to go hunting and they were separated in the woods for a short period of time. Alone, the son then witnessed a deer being chased. It was then picked up by some unseen force which then slammed it so hard against a tree it was killed instantly. The boy was shocked. He then became terrified when the dead deer was then lifted off the ground. It then hovered, levitated in the air and then was heading in his direction, as if being offered to the young hunter as a gift. The reason he was in the forest in the first place. The boy didn't move. He then watched as something invisible carried the deer carcass away. The boy took off and found his father and told him what he had witnessed.

On November 5th, 1977 in Little Eagle, South Dakota there were several Bigfoot sightings involving the local police. This was a scenario where a group of men had chased a Bigfoot at night for several hours and they finally had it cornered, so they thought:

*It was surrounded by the vehicles with their lights blazing, but still, it managed to escape into the brush. A rancher who had joined the hunt was puzzled by its escape. He had heard a noise like someone out of breath, and a pounding like the sound of running feet: "I put my flashlight right where I could plainly hear it, only where it should have been, there was nothing in sight! Now what I'm wondering is, can this thing make itself invisible when things get too close for comfort?"* (131)

Invisibility, believe it or not, is said to be one of the secrets of many secret societies and orders throughout the centuries. Like I mentioned earlier, Native American Shamans were one of these that had the ability to go invisible. Invisibility is actually one of the "mind over matter" abilities of students of Raja Yoga. They are taught how to use paranormal powers called Siddhas. Through deep levels of meditation and training, it is said that they can achieve invisibility.

*"Later in Hinduism, around 700-300 BCE, we find the secret doctrines, called the Upanishads, which were written for students. Within the Upanishads, there is a section called the Yogatattva which gives the rich mystical philosophy of the discipline and theory of practice for attaining knowledge of the essence of God. A serious student of raja yoga was taught that certain supernormal powers, called siddhas were a natural outcome of gaining mastery over one's mind and environment, and were used as valuable indications of the student's spiritual progress.*

*One of these yogic siddhas was human invisibility."* (132)

Sasquatch seems to understand invisible energies and cosmic occurrences. Kewaunee Lasperitis seems to think that since they are always busy and they are always going somewhere, they have a job to do here. He strongly believes that they are involved in working with the earth's energy areas, that as humans, we can't feel or see. They are commonly referred to as "high energy" areas. I am starting to wonder if one of these areas is within Monsterland and Leominster State Forest. My journey through the strange would only get weirder when I had the chance to talk with Mike Paterson of Canada.

# 17

# MARBLES FROM THE OTHER SIDE

In my search to find out if Bigfoot, UFOs, and orbs are or are not connected, I needed to talk with someone that has recently experienced some or all of these things. Is there anyone having "real interactions" with Bigfoot? I believe there is. I also believe that he has compiled some of the best evidence of the existence of Sasquatch. He is also showing us that Sasquatch may be something entirely different than what we think they are. His name is Mike Paterson.

Mike was always open-minded about the existence of Sasquatch. When he had an incident back in October of 2008 with a close vocal encounter, he knew at that very moment, that what he heard could be nothing other than a Sasquatch. It was an experience that would change anyone's perspective. Mike is a wildlife photographer and a lover of the outdoors. He was a skeptic turned "believer" literally overnight with that experience. What started as a wildlife photographer's ultimate quest for the picture of his life, his photographic goal of capturing a picture of a Sasquatch, would suddenly turn his life upside down.

He has been researching, on a regular basis, with the owner of a cottage which is located in Ontario, Canada. The property owner, who has owned the cottage for over 30 years, has wanted to stay anonymous, from the get-go. They are documenting their experiences together. They are having encounters with several Bigfoot in this remote cottage in the woods.

Mike Paterson of Sasquatch Ontario and I arranged for a time to speak over the phone. I have been following his research since he started posting his videos on YouTube. Not only is Mike getting footprint castings, he's getting amazing audio of Sasquatch speaking, yes speaking, and in English! From his research, he has come to the understanding that the Sasquatch are a people and hold abilities beyond our own understanding at this time.

Previously, in the Bigfoot research world, what has been captured on audio of alleged Sasquatches has been howls and whistles like the "Sierra Sounds" recorded in Northern California in the 1970's by Ron Moorehead and Al Berry, while they were researching in the Stanislaus National Forest.

Ron and Al recorded hours of vocalizations as well as something quite remarkable called "Samurai Chatter". It seems to be a language spoken amongst the Bigfoot. From these recordings, a former military crypto-linguist Scott R. Nelson, recognized this "chatter" to be a language and he developed the Sasquatch Phonetic Alphabet. In addition to the amazing audio that Mike has been able to record, where you even hear one of them called, Nephatia call Mike's name, Mike has also captured photographic evidence of the weird phenomena that seems to be a part of the Sasquatch interactions, like strange orbs of light and weird figures.

Watching his videos, listening to the audio, looking at some of these photographs, one of which looks like a white Sasquatch with blue eyes holding the camera up to its eye, you start to realize that this could be groundbreaking stuff. From his interaction with this family of Sasquatch in Ontario, Mike is also receiving hand woven gifts from them, including marbles that materialize from nowhere!

This has been witnessed first-hand by film director Chris Munch, who directed *Letters from the Big Man* and is the creator of the video podcast, *Speaking of Sasquatch*. Chris came to the research location to investigate and experience these things for himself. During one of the nights, Chris was inside the cottage and speaking about the subject of quantum physics. At that very moment, a green marble appeared in front of Chris in mid-air and dropped to his feet! I know that this is hard to swallow. This is something that Mike has experienced inside as well as outside the cottage. Mike has a mason jar on his mantle above the fireplace. It is filled to the top with marbles he has received from his Sasquatch interactions. He has accumulated over 500 of them!

On Sasquatch Ontario's YouTube Page it states:

*A continued insight into the strange world of Sasquatch interaction. This is now a two and a half year developed situation with trust built documenting close interaction with a benevolent family of what we believe to be an ancient people who are beyond our evolution. They hold abilities which allow them to exist in a quantum state. Sentient and highly intelligent living in the balance of all. They seem to understand and have learned how to utilize the laws of the universe. They have evolved down a different path than the human race, a path of enlightenment, far past our own evolution.*

*There's good reason why Sasquatch are a labeled a myth and this situation gives an understanding of why.*

Before the Sasquatch Ontario video entitled *Habituation – Denied and Confirmed*, scrolling text explains their mission statement even further:

*Sasquatch Ontario is dedicated to helping others understand the hidden truth of the Sasquatch people. It's been now over two years since we've started documenting a family of Sasquatch at a private property in Ontario, Canada.*

*With the right intention and approach, we've learned that it's entirely possible to befriend the Sasquatch as they will interact with those they choose, those who have good intentions towards them. (133)*

Is he a hoaxer? Is he telling the truth? If this is real, could Mike Paterson hold some of the answers to this whole puzzle? Mike and I became friends through Facebook awhile back. I reached out to Mike and asked him if he was willing to discuss more about his experiences with me.

I told him I was working on a book about sightings of UFOs, Bigfoots, and Orbs in the area and wanted to know if there might be a connection with all three of these phenomena. One of the best places to start would be to reach out to someone like Mike Paterson who claims to be interacting with a family of Bigfoot and has proclaimed that there is indeed some weirdness that comes with Sasquatch sightings and interactions. Mike agreed to talk with me for the book.

I figured that after an hour of talking with him I would be able to tell if he was lying or not, pick up on little nuances in the conversation. Mike is as down to earth as they come and a very smart guy. From my conversations and chats with him, I feel that he is being sincere. He's not making money on this. In order to do so, his videos would need to be set up for advertising. They were never tied to video advertising on YouTube.

What is Mike doing then? Well, if his actions follow what he says he is doing, then he is trying to share the truth about the existence of what is known as Bigfoot. He's sharing the information as well as the evidence he is gathering with the world at large. By doing this, he is giving some credibility and validity to what others have been experiencing around the country, like Mike Parra, a Bigfoot researcher from Colorado and Rob Riggs, co-author/researcher of the 2014 book *Bigfoot.*

Mike has been spending the past twenty-eight months going to the cottage as often as he can. Although Mike will stay inside the cottage during the winter months, he would pitch a tent outside to entice vocalizations. These vocalizations would happen once he would enter his tent. Every time that he stays out there he is getting interactions. And when I say, "interactions", I am not talking about wood knocks and if you are lucky, a couple of prints. This is where it gets weird.

Mike relayed a story to me regarding his first night visiting the cottage. His plan was to sleep in the tent so that he could scrutinize the situation and find out if they did have any Sasquatch activity going on. Mike had set up the tent in the forest. It was late in the evening when he left the owner and his son inside the cottage to head to his tent for the night. He walked down the one lane gravel road and when he turned to go into the forest where his tent was set up, he saw what looked like a large glowing orange eye. Orange? He barely had any light coming off of the small led flashlight that he carried. It couldn't even reach anywhere he was looking. Mike chuckled nervously to himself, turned around and went back to the cottage and slept on the couch for the night.

It was the very next visit that Mike put his fear aside and started sleeping inside the tent. He was also given a fright that night as well with activity outside his tent almost immediately after settling in for the night.

Since that first night, Mike and the cottage owner have cast dozens of footprints, photographically captured various trackways as well as handprints left on Mike's car. The hair from the arm and hand can be seen leaving an oily impression on the body of the vehicle! In my opinion, he's like the equivalent to Jane Goodall of Sasquatch research. Mike Paterson has a lot of haters in internet land. They feel what he is posting is fake and not real. It can't be true. The truth is stranger than fiction.

RONNY: **What is your background? Born and raised in Canada?**

MIKE: *My background is of Scottish descent with some Aussie in there as well. I was born and raised in Canada, lived here all my life.*

RONNY: **How did you end up being involved with this research?**

MIKE: *I was spending much of my spare time in the forests chasing wildlife and pursuing nature photography. I'd had an epiphany one day about searching for the photo opportunity of a lifetime and started looking into the subject of Sasquatch.*

RONNY: **Did you have a significant event that led you to where you are now?**

MIKE: *I'd made some comment on a YouTube video on Sasquatch at some point and was contacted by someone asking if I'd like to visit an area of previous activity since their proximity to me wasn't too distant. I agreed and it was maybe a month or so later we met up and I was shown the area. We looked for sign and at one point a rock was smacked against a tree by the person I was with. Seconds later all hell broke loose as I heard what sounded just like gorilla chest thumps. I'd spent enough time in the forest at this point to know something felt "off". It was seconds later while standing there listening that the bellow of a Sasquatch rang through the forest with three giant low end guttural whoops. They were very clear, close and extremely loud. I recall at the time saying how it sounded so pronounced that they sounded like they could speak English. Little did I know my life instantly changed at that very moment!*

*I'd had another incident previously camping in another area in the Bon Echo region of Ontario. I was there for a couple nights with a good friend of mine and I was in that mission mode for Sasquatch. That was the very first time I'd gone out looking for them. There's been sightings and activity in the region.*

*I was given a great hardly used camp spot away from everything. It was all bush on the side of the lake we were on. It was about 8 AM the next morning when we heard what sounded like screaming although it didn't sound human. I'm convinced it was a Sasquatch. It sounded similar to a camp tear down video in Sequoia National Park I'd heard after the fact.*

*There was a third incident again giving activity very close the next week after my close vocal encounter. So the very first three times I went looking for Sasquatch, strange things had happened. Seems a little odd that I have three possible incidents during my first three visits looking for activity.*

RONNY: **Do you have any childhood experiences with the paranormal? Orbs? Lights in the sky?**

MIKE: *My mum has told me about things that happened in our home when I was a child. I have no recollection of anything but have been told that yes, we did have some very strange things going on. I've never really noticed orbs or lights in the sky prior to what I'm dealing with right now. I never suspected anything like this would be part of Sasquatch activity when I first got involved and even after spending several years at it. It wasn't until this current situation that all the pieces fell together.*

RONNY: **Do you come from a religious family or one of Christian faith?**

MIKE: *My family's religious beliefs vary and my own belief is of a spiritual nature that there is a higher power although I personally completely disagree with organized religion. I see it as complete hypocrisy and the root cause of many issues within our societies. My personal belief is one on one. I'm always striving for enlightenment and being a better person.*

RONNY: **What do you believe that you are interacting with? Is it an animal? Do you believe that they are inter-dimensional or alien?**

MIKE: *I believe we're dealing with the Sasquatch people. We've seen them in photos, seen their prints, spoken with them, etc. I've learned that Sasquatch are not what most believe them to be. They're far beyond the comprehension of many. As science and organizations continue to try and prove an ape, there's a growing number who are realizing the truth of Sasquatch through their own personal situations. I believe they're a people. They have names, animals don't. While they seem very animalistic, they're far beyond the intelligence that most are aware of.*

*They continually show us their intelligence, their patience, and compassion through interactions and incidents that continually give us insight into their truth. I believe they are inter-dimensional as activity can follow you anywhere. I've had a sign of their presence left inside my locked vehicle on numerous occasions. They've been inside my home and shown their presence through numerous interactions including a mind-blowing telepathic incident one night while I was drifting off on the couch. I was woken by a very prominent front and center grunt inside my head that made him sound like he was standing in the room.*

*When it happens to you, you know it's not your own thoughts, not even close. It was another piece of the puzzle they allow as interactions continue. They're always progressing, showing us new things, new incidents and allowing us more knowledge and insight.*

*We've had several incidents of physical interaction, even on our faces (myself and the owner) and we were both witnesses to the dark strange smoke-like substance that appeared inches from both of our faces immediately prior to being touched. They can move silently. They can stand beside you and you wouldn't even know it or they may allow you to know through some sign they give. Sasquatch are huge on sign. This is what they do for those they interact with. It's a constant leaving or showing of sign revealing their presence. They also seem to work on intent which is a big part of that sign.*

*They may have an alien origin, I don't know. They have abilities that exist on a quantum level. It seems as if they've learned the laws of the universe and that they can possibly exist in multiple realities at the same time. They can manifest matter from seemingly thin air, something we've witnessed a multitude of times at this stage. For instance just last visit, we had marbles appear from thin air in front of my eyes. It seems they're starting to now show more sign in real time in front of our eyes.*

RONNY: **Are there reports of not only orbs but UFOS in your research area in Ontario?**

MIKE: *Not that I'm aware of but I've stated many times to the owner that it wouldn't surprise me at this point to see some UFO activity. We've witnessed a red orb that seems other-worldly that's given us a show on a couple of occasions. That red orb seems alien. It's quite the spectacle being able to change shape, pulsate and move freely about.*

RONNY: **We have seen basketball-sized orbs in Leominster State Forest as well as within the city and according to several people – these are associated with Sasquatch. Do you believe that?**

MIKE: *I definitely think the orb activity is associated with Sasquatch activity. There have been many incidents of seeing lights in the forest as well as the orbs (which could very well be orbs). There's an extreme amount of strangeness that comes with close Sasquatch activity. Anyone that gets close enough would understand. I've spoken with several others around the world that also have activity and are well aware of the*

207

*strangeness that comes with the Sasquatch.*

RONNY: **What do you think the orbs are? Do you believe that the Sasquatch are traveling within these orbs? Are they a phenomenon that is just connected somehow with the Sasquatch?**

MIKE: *Bottom line is I really don't know what orbs are. I can speculate but it's just guessing at this point. What I do know is the phenomenon of the orb activity definitely seems related to Sasquatch activity.*

RONNY: **Is there a well-known mountain or particular legend associated with the Mountain in the area?**

MIKE: *We're not in a mountainous region. Funny how when I first got involved in this subject, most would scoff at any sightings outside a mountainous region. Look at the sightings database of reports now. Oh, how things have changed.*

RONNY: **Are there any signs of high desirable minerals, diamonds, gold, quartz or granite in the research area?**

MIKE: *Ontario is rich in mineral deposits, as well as water, flora, and fauna. With regards to the research area, I prefer to keep certain aspects confidential to minimize intrusion.*

RONNY: **Is your research site on or near Native American land?**

MIKE: *Sorry, again I do not like to give pertinent information that could result in intrusion. We protect this as much as we can and certain information is best kept confidential.*

RONNY: **Reports and experiences of people dealing with invisible Sasquatch? What do you think is going on here? How are they doing this?**

MIKE: *Yes, Sasquatch are invisible, I believe for the most part. They're able to leave footprints in snow when they choose. We've had many incidents of single prints left for us in the snow without track-ways. We've also been witness to literally 100's of prints now into our third winter. 100% of those prints go nowhere. They're all left specifically for us during this continuing situation.*

*As previously mentioned, it seems to me that the Sasquatch have learned the laws of the universe. Maybe their invisibility is due to a frequency, vibration or bending of light. The bottom line is I don't know. If I did know, I don't think I'd be giving that information out. It seems there's another reality within our own, a reality that they seem to exist in for the most part but with the ability to step into and out of our reality at will (in part or in whole). There may be countless realities we're unaware of. Although again, I simply don't know.*

RONNY: **You mentioned in one of your videos about catching an alien and Sasquatch in the same photograph...what is the association with the Greys and the Sasquatch? Are they working together in some capacity?**

MIKE: *The owner and I had a discussion in my vehicle on a drive up to the location one visit. We've learned that they are listening. They can hear our conversations. I would do experiments with the photos saying things like "wouldn't it be amazing to see a picture of a Sasquatch and an alien in the same photograph".*

*That same night I was given just that on my point and shoot camera as it sat inside the cottage on the table. Four photos appeared with a 60-second time frame (all together) between the four shots.*

*One clearly had a stickman figure in front of a large tree that was gone in the other photos. A large dark upright figure changes positions throughout the frames (Sasquatch). An incredible series of photos showing a strange brightly lit forest when the photos were given in complete darkness. The metadata states the flash did not fire. I have no knowledge of greys or any relation to Sasquatch although I have seen a couple of strange things given in drawings and photos that could pertain to some involvement.*

RONNY: **Where do you think your research is headed? Are there plans to capture any of your interactions on film, with some dialogue between the Sasquatch?**

MIKE: *We just roll with it. Whatever happens, happens. There are no expectations. You can't really have expectations with Sasquatch. It doesn't work like that. They make the rules. We'll continue to develop the relationship we've built over the last twenty-eight months and hope that things continue to progress. Nephatia, for the last couple of visits, has spoken to me while I was outside with the video camera running, so his dialogue has been captured on video as well as audio recorders that are strategically placed.*

*It seems that when they do something once, they continue to build rather than step backward. It's a slow but continuous and progressive process that will hopefully yield some incredible insight during the visits. All we can do is keep at it and hope for the best. Being completely honest with them is the way to go in my opinion.*

*They can read our intent and they'll know if you're trying to pull a fast one on them. Their abilities and intelligence are highly underestimated by many on this subject. Those that get it will move forward and possibly gain insight through their own personal interactions with the Sasquatch. Those who continue to chase apes I believe will always stay stagnant in their approach, except for maybe a reaction at times. That seems to be the consensus over the past many decades. I don't think that'll change until one accepts the truth of them and changes their intent and approach.*

I told Mike I would follow up soon with more questions and thanked him for his time. What he is experiencing is fascinating! I felt like I could have talked to him for hours.

Before I hung up with him I asked him for some advice on how to get a Bigfoot to interact with me on my next visit to Leominster State Forest. He told me to be pure of thought when I go in there for hikes, they will know my intentions. Leaving gifts and trying to communicate with them on the mental level even where I sit now can help. As he mentioned, he has had experiences outside of the research area and in his own home...so they don't seem restricted to just the forest. He also remarked that it seems as if they are listening to us.

Wow. I don't think I am going to be able to sleep tonight. If this is real, it's quite remarkable and earth shattering. And if it's real, will it ever be widely accepted as truth? We are supposedly living now in the "Age of Awakening". Could this be one of the truths that we will see if and when the veil is ever lifted?

The search is on for Bigfoot and UFOS and I don't see it stopping. I am just one of many. With all of the new technologies out there, everyone carrying a phone equipped with camera and video, the new discoveries they are making in science, it will just be a matter of time before someone is able to prove without a doubt that they exist. Mike Paterson is helping spearhead that effort. But marbles from the other side? If you are like me, then you need to experience things for yourself to believe if something is real or not. I thought this was cool and scary at the same time.

Since my last conversation with Mike, a few weeks went by and I was able to make it out to Leominster State Forest for a solo hike. I remember what he told me and I made sure that I had been mindful of my attitude and my approach. I scoured the area looking for any signs and checked several trail head openings. I stopped several times, immediately sat down off the trail and just listened quietly. I didn't leave any gifts but did try to evoke a peaceful presence when I was in the woods. What I did notice was that it was dead quiet. Again. There were no birds and no other animals moving about.

I was out for a little over an hour during the afternoon and nothing about the atmosphere of silence changed. It was spooky, to say the least. As I headed back to my car and while I was there kept thinking about Mike's experience and those damn marbles. My mind was spinning. How cool would it be to get a marble from a Sasquatch? Are they regular marbles? Where in the hell are they coming from and is there some significance? The shape? The material?

A few days later, May 7th to be exact, I was out cleaning the front of my yard, doing some raking, planting flowers and spreading mulch. I had just planted some flowers and plants along the driveway. I decided to take a quick five-minute break before I started to mulch the spot. I stopped to take a drink of water and was just reflecting on how beautiful the day was, enjoying the cool breeze, soaking in the sun, remembering all the snow we got hammered with this past winter. I felt really blessed just to be outside enjoying the warm sun, weather, and nature. I was in a tranquil state of mind and I felt overwhelmed with a sense of peace that I haven't felt in quite some time. I felt good. I felt really good.

I went back to the area I was planning to mulch. I did a quick check and made sure that I cleared the area so that there were no weeds or rocks. I was ready to mulch. The last spot I cleared was to be my starting point. I made a mental note, I will start mulching here. I left to go get a bag of mulch from a few yards up the driveway, literally seconds had passed, and when I came back to the same spot, there it was a marble! It was just sitting in the middle of the area and on top of the dirt. It wasn't there before. It was a blue, yellow and clear marble. Right where I was about to start the mulch! I looked around my front yard looking for the culprit. I looked back down and the idea of this thing coming in from another dimension creeped me out. I got the chills.

I couldn't believe my eyes. I picked it up and marveled that it looked just like the photos of the marbles I had seen of Mike Paterson's. The bubbles were visible through the clear sides of the marble. I quickly brought it into my office and put it on my shelf so that it wouldn't be disturbed. I actually put a book in front of it so that no one would move it. I shook my head and went back to work. "No way man, no way", I kept repeating to myself. But the marble was clearly not there in the dirt moments before. How the hell did that just happen? I grabbed my notebook and quickly made note of the time, which was 11:59 AM.

I woke the next morning on May 8th and suddenly remembered the marble. I went to retrieve it from the shelf in my office. When I pulled the marble out again I was shocked a second time because this was a different marble! The clear part of the marble was now a light green and then there was an additional black line along with a red one and the original yellow line in the marble! I glanced down at my phone and noted the time. It was 12:22 PM. I was so mad that I didn't take a picture of the marble before I put it on the shelf. I said out loud in my office to no one, "Okay, send me another one so that I can take a picture of it." Great, now I am talking to myself and getting marbles from Bigfoot land. But I remembered what Mike said to me over the phone *"they found out that they (Sasquatch) are listening to them."* I was hoping they would hear me.

I reluctantly told my wife about my conversations with Mike and the sequence of events leading up to what happened. She just looked at me and nodded her head.

I told her that the marble was definitely not there before and shared what Mike Paterson has been experiencing with receiving these marbles. I said out loud "I want to get another one so that I could take a picture of it as soon as I get it so that I could see if it changes". I believe my wife's response had something to do with me losing "my marbles" and she walked off. Officially losing my mind.

The next day, May 9th, I headed over to my parent's house to help them move some furniture. As my father and I were walking in from the garage and walking into the doorway leading into the house, my father walking before me, stopped over the door mat and said, "Look out, there's a marble right there...not sure how that got there".

I had goosebumps. My father continued into the house. As I walked through the doorway I looked down. I stopped dead in my tracks. Wedged between the door mat and the step plate, in the center of it was a blue and clear marble (picture at beginning of chapter). The marble was wedged between the two almost as if to keep it securely in place. My heart skipped a beat. I quickly rubbed my eyes and reached down, continued to look at it and noticing the clear part with bubbles exposed. I put it in my pocket and moved on, trying to conceal my excitement. Glancing at the phone and noting that the time was 11:15 AM. I did find it curious that the times that these marbles were found were somewhat similar. I will have to ask Mike Paterson about this the next time we speak and if there is any correlation.

That following Monday, May 11th, I went for another hike, this time on the Fitchburg side of Notown Reservoir. That weekend we had some family over for a cookout. My wife and I had cleared an area where we are going to be putting some cobblestone pavers down for a fire pit. During the middle of her conversation, she looks down and sees an orange marble just sitting on top of the dirt.

She yelled to me to come quick and I picked it up. It was clean as a whistle. It was placed there and not dug up from the dirt. She looked at me amazingly with her eyes widening "That was not there a minute ago! I swear to God. I was looking over in this direction and looked back and it was just there. It just appeared out of nowhere! That is weird!" said Amy.

Amy looked at me and I could see that her mind was starting to turn quickly. Coincidence? It is only three marbles.

For me to believe that this isn't just a coincidence, I need to see more than three. But if I get five, do I need ten? If I get ten, do I need twenty to believe? I can't remember that last time I found a marble, let alone three, especially after talking with someone about their significance with the phenomenon and my goal of receiving them...nope, I don't think I ever have! Seems odd to me that this is exactly what Mike Paterson told me he has experienced and now it's happening over here!? So far, just these three marbles, but maybe there are more on the way with each visit to the forest. I have a Mason jar ready in case they keep on coming.

I have seen the orange orbs numerous times, seen a trackway and cast a footprint of a potential Bigfoot in Leominster State Forest. I have seen UFOs in Canada when I was a child and here in Leominster and central Massachusetts. I am not the only one seeing these things. Some people are willing to share, others will not and some may take their experience and stories to their graves. This has been going on for hundreds of years and it seems to be taking place in the same areas, year after year. Why is that?

# 18

# IS LEOMINSTER STATE FOREST A SACRED PLACE?

Are areas where UFOs, Bigfoot, and Orbs are found sacred? Within UFO and Bigfoot sightings, "High Strangeness" seems to follow suit. These are paranormal events that seem to surround UFO activity and include the appearance of humanoid creatures, electromagnetic effects, unusual sounds and poltergeist activity. There are also reports of strange light phenomena, the appearance of phantom-like entities and lastly a variety of psychic phenomena.

Most Bigfoot researchers will leave out or ignore these types of phenomena because it doesn't coincide with their beliefs in that this is a flesh and blood animal that they are chasing. Not to mention, the apprehension of sharing these details for fear of being ridiculed. This has been echoed throughout the book from other researchers.

But we can't ignore all these "strange events" surrounding Sasquatch encounters. They seem to be connected as others have discovered areas that have Bigfoot sightings also have UFO sightings and vice versa. Could these Bigfoots, UFOs and supernatural phenomena all be coming from the same place?

Places like the Bridgewater Triangle and October Mountain that have all of this strange phenomena were once areas that were inhabited by the Native Americans of the day. Some of these areas were cursed by the Native Americans due to the unfair treatment that they received from the white colonists. Also due to a number of deaths that occurred to their people like in Hockomock Swamp during King Philip's War, some believe that this has created "negative energy" in these areas.

The Native Americans considered certain areas that they inhabited magical and sacred. But why? Aside from being their headquarters or hunting grounds, what do these places contain that would make them so special? More people are aware of this strange center of activity in Massachusetts and some are not. One wonders, like the other areas that were deemed sacred and magical, if the Leominster area was also cursed when sold from the Native Americans to the white settlers?

An area of about eighty square miles, which was inhabited and owned by Sholan, Sachem of the Nashaways, was deeded to two settlers in 1642. It would eventually become the town of Lancaster in 1645.

An additional tract of land, known as "Lancaster New" would eventually become Leominster in 1740, named after Leominster, England. Lancaster was the site of the Mary Rowlandson (1637-1711) attack in February of 1676 during King Philip's War. It was fought partially in Lancaster, where a tribe of several hundred Indians pillaged the entire town. Mrs. Rowland was kidnapped and eventually released months later at what is known as "Redemption Rock" in Princeton near Leominster State Forest. (134)

The areas of Lancaster and in the neighboring town of Sterling were considered sacred by the local Native Americans. The headquarters of the Nashaways was located between Wauschacum Ponds in Sterling. This area is within close proximity to Leominster State Forest and Monsterland.

According to *Native American Place Names* by R.A. Douglas-Lithgow originally published in 1909, Wauschacum means, "The Sea". There are two bodies of water, East Wauschacum Pond, and West Wauschacum Pond. These ponds are connected via the Wauschacum brook.

This a beautiful area where I personally go fishing and it is a great place to go kayaking. The tribe held councils here and the grounds around the lake were devoted to Indian sports, games and "regattas" which were held on the waters of the lake. There was an Indian church on the grounds as well. This body of water had its share of death and its place in history.

According to the 1891 book *Leominster Traditions* by William A. Emerson:

> *"In May of 1776, the first naval battle on the inland waters of Massachusetts was fought at Wauschacum. Captain Henchman when marching towards the Connecticut valley was informed that there was a party of hostile Indians at this lake. He turned hither and surprised a party in their canoes taking fish. He led an instant attack upon them, killing seven and taking twenty-nine prisoners." (135)*

The immediate area has a history of unrest and death. I also uncovered something interesting that is found in the area, Chiastolite. Chiastolite is only found in a few places on our planet. This stone is found mainly in Mariposa, California, the Henan province of China and a few localities within Southern Australia. In Massachusetts, it has been found in Westford, Clinton, Sterling, Leominster, and Lancaster along the Lancaster drumlines known as George and Ballard Hill. Aside from its limited locations where it can be found, what makes this stone unique is what it is said to be able to do.

Chiastolite is a form of the mineral Andalusite that contains black particles of graphite arranged in geometric patterns. The graphite is pushed aside by crystal growth within a rock that is being metamorphosed. As growth occurs, the particles become concentrated at crystal interfaces. The result can be a cross-shaped pattern within the mineral – also called the cross stone.

People have known about these cross stones for centuries and have valued them for their perceived religious or spiritual meaning. This unusual stone is regarded as a highly protective stone, and these ancient beliefs have somehow proven themselves correct due to the psychic abilities that this stone possesses. It is supposed to contain a highly protective vibration. The local Indians would wear it as protective jewelry as they went into battle.

When it comes to New Age and crystals, Chiastolite is also considered one of the best crystals for psychic resistance. It helps the wearer to intensify his channeling abilities in the course of contacting the spirit world. It also has a strong relationship with the phase of death and rebirth and can assist with the acceptance and reception of a life beyond. The cross-shaped formation on Chiastolite is believed to be the art of God himself. Said to provide protection from the "evil eye", the crystal is also believed to be a "bridge" for "crossing over" to the "other side" and can be useful in both astral and mind travel.

The stone is also said to have strong metaphysical properties. It has the ability to assist one during meditation and it will aid you in connecting with the Akashic records to discover past life information. The Akashic records are said to contain everything that has occurred to humanity since the beginning of time. Think of it as one big computer holding all the data of the universe, like the DNA of the universe. It is also considered to be what Christians call "The Everlasting Book of Life".

It is believed that the Akashic Records are the individual records of a soul from the time it leaves its point of origin until its return. At the time we make the decision to experience life as an independent entity, there is a field of energy created to record every thought, word, emotion, and action generated by that experience. That field of energy is the Akashic Records. Akashic because it is composed of Akasha, (the energetic substance from which all life is formed); and Records because its objective is to record all life experience. (136)

So we have a unique stone, found only in a few places across our globe that is supposed to enable one to access the spirit world. If this stone is that special, then one would assume that the area where it originates must be considered sacred or special as well.

These special or sacred places also have another identification of stone, a much larger one. These sacred areas contain megalithic structures as well as stone chambers and or ancient stone sites. When I say megalithic, I am referring to the erection of large stone columns such as those found at Stonehenge in England and Carnac in France.

We still don't know what they were used for and we are still trying to figure out who built them. There are over two hundred stone chamber or structure locations throughout New England that have been uncovered by the New England Antiquities Research Association, which is based in Worcester, Massachusetts.

The Native Americans, the Pequots of Southern New England believed that these areas containing these megaliths and stone sites were indeed sacred. In the book *Ancient Stone Sites*, an interesting fact emerges that *"Celtic monasteries were built on sacred ground, including locations that were holy to pre-*

*Christian traditions. To the Celtic mind, if the Pequots considered the area sacred, as suggested by the supernatural legends of the area, what better place to build a monastery?"* (137)

The "supernatural legends of the area" sounds like what Leominster residents have been seeing and experiencing for a very long time. With the culmination of UFOs, Bigfoot sightings, orange orbs and ghosts, I am convinced that Leominster State Forest is one of these sacred places.

We seem to have all the ingredients necessary in the Leominster area for it to contain a sacred site. Although a stone chamber or structure has not been officially discovered in Leominster State Forest, it could still be there lying in wait for someone to come along and discover it.

But something interesting was found in Leominster State Forest...in the area of Notown reservoir, a stone table, which some believe to be a sacrificial table. But how does this tie in with a sacred site? The stone table has a remarkable resemblance to one that was found at a famous stone chamber. It is the same kind of table that was found north in Salem, New Hampshire at what is known as "Mystery Hill".

Mystery Hill is considered American's Stonehenge. No one really knows who built these stone chambers. The likely suspects are the Phoenicians, the Culdee Monks, the Vikings, as well as the early indigenous people. Some believe that they were here long before the Native Americans. Mystery Hill, at the very least, is most likely the oldest man-made construction in the United States.

The discovery of a possible sacrificial table found off of Granite Street entrance of Leominster State Forest back in the 1970's, when it then mysteriously disappeared for almost thirty years and finally resurfaced, tells me that the possibility exists of Leominster being one of these special places. A high probability. The stone has been dubbed the Notown Table Stone. The stone is currently on display in front of the Leominster Historical Society's headquarters on School Street in Leominster.

Some speculate that the area of Notown Reservoir is a sacred place due to the discovery of the stone, chiastolite, and the phenomena that have plagued the area for a very long time. What's interesting is that the Notown Table Stone was found off of Granite Street, near the site of where the Bigfoot tracks were located.

In July of 1974 in the Worcester Telegram and Gazette, there was an article entitled *No Town Rock Stirs Interest in Prehistory*, which sheds some light on the No Town Table stone:

> *Did ancient civilizations similar to those found in Europe at the time of Stonehenge once settle in the Notown area of Leominster? This question and many others are pondered by the Leominster Historical Society and Wallace C. Nash of Stagecoach Road. Nash discovered almost two years ago a slab similar in appearance to a sacrificial stone at Mystery Hill in North Salem, NH. Officials at Mystery Hill became interested in Nash's find and asked him to return to photograph the huge rock. Nash returned last week but all he found were marks where the huge rock had been dragged off.*

William Nash, who was twenty-seven years old at the time and one who knew the woods well, made an incredible find. He was a hunter and worked for his father, who owned the Nash Detective Agency. The stone, which was on state-owned land, was dragged off and had subsequently disappeared. Nash estimated that the stone had to be about 600 to 900 pounds in weight. It would be very difficult to move without the aid of machinery. Mystery Hill officials were extremely excited about the find in Leominster. But who took the stone?

> "We don't want anyone to think they are in trouble if they took the stone. We just want them to let us know they have it," he said. Nash said there is a "strong coincidence" about the stones on Mystery Hill which is located just north of Lawrence, and the Notown rock. He went to Mystery Hill and talked with Mystery Hill Corp. President Robert Stone. The sacrificial stone in New Hampshire looked like the one he saw in the woods off Granite Street and Mt. Elam Road here. Nash didn't recognize the importance of his discovery when he first saw it while grouse hunting. "I was curious, though because it had an unusual groove around it." Sacrificial stones have those grooves to catch the blood.

Nash believes that the stone was used for animal sacrifices, not human. His theory is based on the fact that there was evidence of stone pens and feeding bins north at Mystery Hill which contained and housed the animals that were to be eventually sacrificed. He doesn't say if these pens were also found in Leominster. Radiocarbon tests at Mystery Hill and a new method of cross-checking the carbon date with tree borings show the area was built about 2,000 BC. This would put Mystery Hill at the same time as the stone building in Europe and possibly in Leominster. There were signs of large bonfires that were found in the Monoosnock Hill area of Leominster, similar to those found at Mystery Hill.

At Mystery Hill, there is a man-made cave. It is rumored that there could be one hidden away somewhere near Monoosnock Hill possibly facing Mt. Wachusett, which was also considered another sacred place by the Native Americans. The theory of the Culdee monks being responsible for these stone chambers has some validity to it. The article continues saying.

> *The theory of the Culdee Monks has interested the local society because another stone with strange markings has also been seen in Notown. A photograph of the stone was featured in a 1946 book called "The Ruins of Great Ireland in New England." No one has seen the strange stone in years, though. Nash said there are many odd relics in the Notown area, but they are largely inaccessible because of the terrain. (138)*

In the 2006 book *Ancient Stone Sites of New England and the debate over Early European Exploration,* author David Goudsward talks about the Notown Table Stone:

> *"Despite the uproar about the stone's discovery, disappearance, and reappearance, it was not the stone's first time in the spotlight. The 1946 publication of William B. Goodwin's Culdee Monk theory included a vast network of Missionary outposts radiating out of his stone village in North Salem. The Notown grooved rock, per Goodwin's theory, "was the ceremonial center for an outpost in Leominster." Primary evidence of this colony was the grooved slab, as well as a small boulder with pictographs, a stone wall leading from the grooved stone on the hilltop to a water supply in the valley below and the proximity to the Mohican Trail. (139)*

There is a strong belief that the rocks and megaliths were placed in these areas to mark them due to the high energy that these areas produced. Others feel that the stones, quartz and or granite of these rocks help with creating some type of high energy. What was that high energy used for?

Mystery Hill is a giant megalithic astronomical complex

constructed sometime during the Bronze Age. There is evidence that the stone chambers and megaliths that are found in these areas are also astronomically aligned. The sunrise and sunset of the equinoxes and solstices, the North Star as well as lunar alignments. Phil Imbrogno in *Celtic Mysteries in New England* backs up this claim:

> *"The Winter Solstice Sunset Monolith at Mystery Hill was the first stone suspected to have solar alignment. The stone marker was placed at the most southerly point of the setting sun almost 4,000 years ago but is off today because of a change in the direction that the earth points to in space. This wobbling of the earth's orbit is called "precession of the Equinox" and is the reason why every several thousand years we have a new 'North Star"* (140)

The Celts believed that when the soul left this earth it traveled on a westerly course to follow the setting sun. Imbrogno surmises that this may be why many of the chambers point to the east, representing birth, and to the west, representing death. (141)

Carl Barton, a Yale graduate and retired geologist also believes that the stone chambers are situated over areas of high energy and that they were used by a very ancient people as temples. (142)

Carl believes that the temples were built by a society of mythical proportions. He believes that many of the structures were the product of the Atlanteans who fled to North America after the sinking of their continent! Yes, the fabled city of Atlantis that the philosopher Plato talked about. Not everyone believes that the Atlanteans are the ones who built the temples, but some believe that they did have an integral part in identifying these high energy areas. It is assumed that the reasons that the rocks and megaliths were placed in these areas was to mark them. Phil Imbrogno explains further:

*"The people of Atlantis did not build the chambers, but they marked the areas of "high energy" with standing stones. These standing stones harnessed the energy from the earth and focused it. Later, when the area was explored by the Celts, they found these areas of high energy still marked by the standing stones and built temples over them... The energy that these stone chambers seem to emit has a greater effect on people who are empaths or who have other psychic abilities."* (143)

Others feel that the stones, quartz and or granite of these rocks help with creating some type of strong energy. An energy so strong that there are those who believe that these sacred sites are a gateway or a portal to another dimension or world! If there is a portal somewhere within Leominster State Forest, this could be where all of the different phenomena is emanating from.

Carl also believes that the Phoenicians are the ones that built the stone chambers and that earth's energy field in these locations was much stronger at one point in time since all the chambers were aligned through magnetic lines of force. The chambers were portals to the other side and were used for traveling out of the body. People would come to these chambers to talk with loved ones who had passed over.

In the 2015 book *Bigfoot* by Tom Burnette and Rob Riggs, the co-authors' Bigfoot research focuses on the Big Thicket region of Texas. They had this to say about these energy areas and their astrological significance,

*"Some ancient cultures, particularly among the native peoples of the Americas and Celtic Europe, seemed to have*

been attuned to the mysteries of strange lights and subtle energies. They were very concerned about identifying places where these energy fields were said to periodically focus and attached great importance to the astrological significance of the equinoxes and solstices in predicting when the focusing effect would occur. Some scholars think such cultures believed the times and places this occurred provided temporary openings between this world and other realities. Curiously, for reasons which remain essentially unknown, they also built long, perfectly straight roads or lines, sometimes called ley lines connecting these places to their cultural and ceremonial centers" (144)

There were a lot of UFO sightings during 1983 to 1995 in the Hudson Valley of New York. In the book entitled *Celtic Mysteries of New England* by Philip Imbrogno, the author notes that *"in the counties of Putnam and Westchester, there are American Indian legends of magical and sacred places, they believed were gateways to another world."* (145)

In regards to the stone chambers of Hudson Valley, a neighbor of John Brendt remembers hearing stories about strange lights around the chambers from his grandfather. He said according to legends, the chambers were built by the Druids who colonized the area over 4,000 years ago. The lights are said to be captured spirits of the Indians who the Druid priests sacrificed in these chambers. (146)

There is a domed mountain in New York called Ninham Mountain. It is composed of many types of granite and a great number of minerals, including quartz, feldspar, garnet, mica and magnetite. It's the highest point in the area and has a federal government and state police antenna "farm" on the peak, transmitting communication between all law enforcement agencies throughout the southern part of New York.

The Ninham Mountain is named after Daniel Ninham, the last great Native American sachem or chief of the Wappinger tribe. The Ninham Mountain *"was very important to them and it was considered a sacred place where the spirits connected with our world. As recently as the last century, shamans would climb to the mountain's top to meditate and enter trances to meet with the spirits of light that lived there."* (147)

I began to ponder the possibility of some type of portal located within Leominster State Forest. This could very well define why the area was considered sacred or special. Author Imbrogno believes that it is entirely possible that we don't have to reach the speed of light to escape our bubble universe. If space can be warped, by an electromagnetic pulse, it could create a sort of wormhole or tunnel to the fourth dimension. The chambers in New England may, in fact, be the "energy generators" that accomplish this, making interdimensional travel possible. (148)

He continues, "Time-Dilation - theoretically, once you cross the fourth dimension, you once again enter linear time in another universe. The evidence suggests that UFOs may be using the location of the chambers as sort of a doorway into their universe."(147) Phil Imbrogno also believes "Some of the chambers may be totally engulfed in a time distortion effect and when the field is activated, the entire chamber itself may vanish and then reappear! In this case, the chamber itself could act as a vehicle to transport people to this other world. (149)

Other researchers have suggested this theory that UFOs are coming in and out of our dimension. I had a friend, while in New England viewing the night sky, with a spectacular view from his bedroom, witnessed what looked like a circle in the sky open up followed by a myriad of colors and a dirigible-like craft emerged. There was a flame behind the craft as if it had turned its afterburner on and then the "hole" closed up. The craft flew away from view. Dr. Matthew A Johnson, a psychiatrist, and Bigfoot researcher, while researching in Oregon, recently witnessed a portal open up at their research area and watched a Sasquatch walk out of the portal. The portal then closed up behind him!

Researcher John A. Keel noticed something he termed as "windows" when he went looking for patterns in UFO sightings. Similar to the straight lines that French Researcher Aime Michel claimed he had discovered of the French sightings from the 1950's.

From John Keel's book *Operation Trojan Horse*:

*"Sightings within a given area during a specific period of time were confined to sectors with a radius of about 200 miles. The objects sometimes do follow a straight course within these sectors, but they vanish (or no reports are received) outside of the 200-mile boundary...every state in the United States has from two to ten "windows." These are areas where UFOs appear repeatedly year after year. The objects will appear in these places and pursue courses throughout the 200-mile limitation. These window areas seem to form larger circles of activities. The great circle from Canada (not to be confused with the traditional geographic Great Circle) in the northwest through the Central States and back into northeast Canada is a major window. Hundreds of smaller windows lie inside that circle...many windows center directly over areas of magnetic deviation...UFOs seem to congregate above the highest available hills in these window areas. They become visible in these centers and then radiate outward, traveling sometimes 100 to 200 miles before disappearing again."*
*(150)*

If UFOs are congregating above the highest available hills in these "window areas" then the South Monoosnoc Hill is the highest point in the city of Leominster at 1,020 feet. This is the same location of the supposed hidden cave that Nash suspects has been undiscovered and is facing Mt. Wachusett. Leominster could very well be one of these window areas. I asked myself if there might be some significant reason why this undiscovered cave would be facing the mountain. It could be facing in the direction of Wachusett Reservoir. It has been rumored that grey aliens have been sighted peaking behind and running in between the neat rows of planted trees along the reservoir.

My wife Amy used to work in West Boylston and had an amazing view of Wachusett Reservoir. She witnessed a green ball of light, descend from the sky and shoot straight down into the Reservoir. She has witnessed this twice. There were witnesses with her on both occasions. The green light came from the same area above the reservoir and entered the same point in the water both times. Completely silent. The first time she held up her cell phone to take a picture because she thought that this light, possibly a plane, was going to crash. Her cell phone, which had a full battery, suddenly went dead when she pointed it in the direction of the falling light. It entered the water without a splash or a visible wake.

She then recounted to me that she has witnessed this green light before when she was a child. She saw it descend in the same way and enter another body of water. She was with her entire family when she was really young camping at Crystal Lake near Wachusett Reservoir. When driving home together from a friend's wedding in Gardner along Route 2, I had the sunroof open and it was midnight. I looked up through the sunroof as did Amy at the same time and I said how cool it would be to see something right now. At that very moment, a green fireball streaked across the center of the sunroof.

Someone was listening.

From the book *Merging Dimensions: The Opening Portals of Sedona,* authors Linda Bradshaw and Tom Dongo state that after ten years of research into the paranormal and UFO full-time, they have come to the conclusion that along with the world-famous vortexes of Sedona, there are also interdimensional portals in the area. There's the possibility that there are sites like this throughout the United States as well as the world. Maybe right here in Massachusetts.

> *"These portals or windows, seem to be entry and exit points into another dimension or universe or place that we, at this point, don't fully understand. This sort of thing isn't only happening in Sedona. Around the world there are a number of these anomalies developing, or, perhaps better put, just being discovered. My estimate would be that there are probably hundreds of these portal-type anomalies spread around the globe.* (151)

It sounds like science fiction, but if there are portals throughout the globe, this could be why people are seeing UFOs, thunderbirds, big black cats, Bigfoot and other creatures. It would explain why these phenomena can disappear and why no one has been able to kill or capture any of these creatures. These portals could be within the places that were considered "sacred" by the First Nations people. Or they could also be in places considered "cursed".

The theory that certain geographical areas are prone to paranormal activity has been suggested long ago. Researcher of the strange, Charles Fort, wrote about this in his book *Lo!.* When discussing a sudden disappearance, he speculated that there may indeed exist a "transporting current" through so-called solid substances, which opens and then closes. It may be that what we call substance is much more open than it is closed.

In other words, Fort was talking about holes in the universe. Various writers have used other labels to describe these holes. New England horror visionary H.P. Lovecraft discussed "dimensional gateways", Rod Serling called them "twilight zones" and Zoologist Ivan T. Sanderson introduced the slightly more ominous term "vile vortices". (152)

Some people believe that there is an invisible "energy grid" that surrounds the planet earth. What makes up this grid is a series of "ley lines". It is believed that early humans were aware of these energy lines due to the fact that modern day humans have found ancient stone sites that line up with these lines.

Where these lines intersect, these "grid points" are considered to contain the highest level of energy, making them "power spots". Ancient humans marked these locations and considered these places to be sacred. They were marked with henges, mounds, megaliths and pyramids. Famous energy vortexes and places of worship, like cathedrals have been located directly above these intersections. Some different "power spots" are in places like Machu Picchu, the Great Pyramids of Giza, Easter Island, and Stonehenge.

There are various Ley Line Grid maps. Ivan T. Sanderson, whose term "vile vortices" was used to describe these lines, mapped out twelve key locations across the planet. All of these sights shared similar qualities, almost all of which were negative. The highlight spots were the Bermuda Triangle and the Devil's Sea.

There is a 480-acre ranch property called "Skinwalker Ranch" in Utah that has been a hotbed for UFOs, Bigfoot creatures, and paranormal activity. More cattle mutilations, strange lights in the sky and odd happenings. The Sherman's, who have now since sold the property to Billionaire Robert Bigelow, have even witnessed strange lights in the sky that seemed to have emerged from orange, circular doorways that appear in midair.

Author and researcher John Keel wrote about this "doorway" theory in his book entitled *Mysterious Beings*, which detailed the strange creatures people were seeing near these UFO hotspots:

> *"These creatures and strange events, seem to occur and recur in the same area year after year, even century after century. This, in itself, indicates that the creatures somehow line up in those areas we call "windows". West Virginia has many unusual creature reports before "Mothman" appeared in 1966...Posses, experienced hunters, and even helicopters have searched for these monsters immediately after some of these events and have failed to find any trace of a hiding space. So where did they go? The sudden appearances and disappearances of these wild, unknown creatures, all over the world, in densely populated areas, suggests that they have some means of transportation or else they are deliberately dumped here and retrieved by some form of transportation. Although UFOs are frequently seen in these same "window" areas, they too, manage to appear and disappear before the bewildered eyes of Air Force Fighter pilots." (153)*

Are we messing with something that we shouldn't be? Scientists at the Large Hadron Collider have been working on trying to detect or even create miniature black holes. The "atom smasher" at the CERN center in Geneva, Switzerland, will be fired up to its highest energy levels ever. It is possible that a completely new universe will be revealed which could rewrite history. The possibility also exists for gravity from our own universe to "leak" into this parallel universe. They were successful in proving the existence of the Higgs Boson, otherwise known as "the God Particle", which is believed to be a key building block of the universe. (154)

We may be starting to see some of these parallel universes bleeding into our own. Fata Morgana is an optical illusion that occurs on land or sea and involves the optical distortion and inversion of distant objects such as boats, which can appear as skyscrapers. This is because the images become stacked when rays of light bend as they pass through the air of different temperatures such as in a heat-haze. The name is derived from Morgan Le Fay, a powerful enchantress from the tales or King Arthur. There was a belief that these mirages which were often seen in the Strait of Messina, were fairy castles in the air or false land created by her witchcraft to lure sailors to their deaths. (155)

Fata Morgana occurs when the Sun heats up a layer of the atmosphere but the layer of air below it remains cool. It creates a temperature inversion. Normally, the air is usually warmer close to the surface, and cooler high up. Layers can develop, each with its own temperature and density. The light then hits a boundary between layers of the atmosphere and becomes refracted or bent and enters the next layer at a different angle. In calm weather, a layer of significantly warmer air can rest over the colder dense air, forming an atmospheric duct which acts like a refracting lens which will then produce a series of inverted and erect images. (156)

A recent example of this occurred in the month of October 2015 in China. Chinese TV news reports have told how thousands of residents in two areas reported separately seeing a huge city form in the skies. This was recorded by many of the onlookers as towering buildings, looking like skyscrapers, appeared in the clouds. There were thousands of people who reportedly saw this city floating over Foshan in The Guangdong province of China. There was also a similar cloud city that emerged a few days later in the province of Jiangxi, China. (157)

This phenomenon reportedly occurred several years ago in China sometime in 2011. There have been suggestions that this could be some sort of hologram or even the emergence of a parallel universe from behind the veil. (158)

There were hundreds of witnesses to a floating cloud-like city above an African Village in Nigeria. It was in a local border village called Dulali. The cloud slowly flew over the village at the height of an average tree. The sounds of machines making noise were heard emanating from the floating city! Almost the entire village witnessed this spectacular event. (159)

We are quick to dismiss stories of this nature because of how easy it may be to manipulate images or video. This reminds me of the Mystery Airship sightings of 1897 and 1909 where people saw these large craft floating above them with the sounds of machinery being heard below by witnesses.

NASA recently confirmed the existence of hidden portals in Earth's magnetic field. These portals are potentially wormholes. The wormholes are associated with Earth's North and South poles. These wormholes could lead into another universe or dimension. These could also explain the unusual disappearances of aircraft and the sudden appearances of UFOs and Bigfoot-like creatures. It is surmised that UFO craft are entering and exiting through portals that are associated with these wormholes.

These portals, which have been a topic of science fiction, are an opening in space or time that connects travelers to distant realms. Jack Scudder, A NASA-funded researcher at the University of Iowa, has figured out how to find these portals. They are being referred to as "X-Points" or "Electron Diffusion Regions". They are located where the magnetic field of Earth connects to the magnetic field of the Sun, creating an uninterrupted path leading from our own planet to the Sun's atmosphere which is 93 million miles away.

They are reported to open and close dozens of times a day. This has been witnessed by NASA's THEMIS Spacecraft and Europe's Cluster probes. These "X-Points" are located a few tens of thousands of kilometers from the earth where the geomagnetic field meets onrushing solar wind. Magnetic portals are invisible, unstable and elusive. They open and close without warning. They form through the process of magnetic reconnection. The lines of magnetic force from the sun and the Earth criss-cross and join and create the "X-Point" where this criss-cross takes place. (160)

If there are portals that have been discovered above the earth's atmosphere, it is quite possible that they exist like the ancients have said across the planet on the ground level. Maybe we are starting to see the "changes" that have been prophesized to occur. Parallel universes could possibly already be starting to make their appearance.

# CONCLUSION

*"It's either, literally physical; or it's in the spiritual in another realm, the unseen realm. What we seem to have no place for—or we have lost the place for—are phenomena that can begin in the unseen realm, and cross over and manifest and show up in our literal physical world...it's both literally, physically happening to a degree; and it's also some kind of psychological, spiritual experience occurring and originating perhaps in another dimension. And so the phenomenon stretches us, or it asks us to stretch to open to realities that are not simply the literal physical world, but to extend to the possibility that there are other unseen realities from which our consciousness, our, if you will, learning processes over the past several hundred years have closed us off."*

- *Dr. John E. Mack – Psychiatrist – Harvard Medical School*

I never expected to write a book. It has been brewing in my mind for several years. I have been a little reluctant to share my own story for fear of ridicule. Not sure what the tipping point was that put me into action, but a sense that someone or something has been trying to show me something, trying to teach me something by opening doors, sending synchronistic signs and developing new friendships has driven me. Everything happens for a reason.

UFOS, Orange Orbs and Bigfoot seem to be cut from the same cloth. I am also convinced beyond a doubt that they are connected. They have been seen together. They also seem to be using the same means to get here. Shamanism. It would seem that the Native American Shamans had otherworldly insight and abilities that we have since lost. The path continues to stretch forward and this seems to be an element on the road to understanding. Consciousness. Quantum Physics. These are the focal points moving forward as well. All of the world's religions speak of transformation. Transforming our being, our soul into something of substance and purpose. Just because we ignore the truth, doesn't mean it goes away or doesn't exist. We must follow our own path.

After reading about the countless stories that involved all of these type of phenomena, my personal experiences with the phenomena and talking with others who have experienced the same thing, the "Interdimensional Bigfoot Theory", surprisingly does make some sense. If the Smithsonian Institution isn't harboring the bones of Bigfoot, keeping the secret safe, then where are the bones? Maybe they just simply come in and go as they please through interdimensional doorways, not staying long to get caught, if that is even possible.

The ability to leave a single footprint or just a few and no other tracks lend credence to their interdimensional nature. The ability to make matter appear out of thin air, responding to intent and interacting with us as if from another realm proves that this is more than just an animal.

There are stories of encounters that continue to expand worldwide where people have experienced these supernatural feats firsthand. Witnesses over the years have seen Sasquatch vanish with a flash in front of their eyes. These monsters have been chased and cornered only to disappear into thin air. They have been seen exiting a UFO, walking out of a portal and following people home from the woods, entering their homes in the spirit form. Spooky stuff. The "High Strangeness" that envelops the mystery of Sasquatch and the strange synchronicities that occur tilt your thinking towards accepting the possibility that this isn't an animal at all, but some type of advanced and evolved human being. There is a pattern amongst researchers who have been chasing an animal for a majority of their life only to come to the conclusion that this is something beyond their grasp and beyond our current understanding. It is not an animal, it is something else.

Sasquatch is a long lost tribe, hidden from sight, dwelling in the dark forests that we dare to enter now in droves. As suggested by Kewaunee, the Sasquatch are working with energy and in these high energy areas. They seem to be the guardians of the forest protecting these sacred locations. It is believed that at one point in time, the various high energy places, these portal sites were all connected.

What if during this Age of Awakening we are heading towards a time where these energy sites will be reconnected with one another? Does this need to happen in order for humanity to elevate and to be enlightened? Does this need to transpire in order for the "others" to enter this realm? It is believed that there is going to be a global shift in human consciousness and the veil will be lifted. The truth will be revealed. But what is that truth?

There are individuals across the world like Mike Paterson and others who are having incredible interactions with the Sasquatch. The message is the same one that has been echoed for eons. We are killing the planet. We are killing ourselves. The messages of love, unity, and interconnectedness are resonating with people who are having these encounters. There is currently a surge and a sense of urgency to reconnect with Mother Nature in order for us to understand our spiritual roots. The universe is connected, it's alive and it's interacting with us. There was someone from long ago that seemed to embody the unification of nature and the universe. He was from Leominster.

John Chapman, aka Johnny Appleseed, was known to wear a pot on his head. But what many people don't know is what he kept under it. Books. The books of one Emanuel Swedenborg. Johnny Appleseed believed that everything had a spirit. The trees, the grass, even mosquitos. There is a story how he put out a fire that he started to keep warm so that the mosquitos swarming his head wouldn't be harmed by the flames and smoke. He cried for days when he was clearing a field and cut a snake in half. He wouldn't graft an apple tree as this would cause harm. He was known by the Native Americans as being a white sachem.

He was loyal to the colonists and befriended the various tribes as well. They proclaimed that he knew the woods better than most of the tribes in the area. He would walk around barefoot and when he was traveling, planting apple trees for various properties along the eastern states, he would often stay at various locations for the night. They would give him food and offer him a bed, but he would refuse to sleep inside. He would prefer to sleep under the stars or with the animals in the barn. He would then give his hosts "A message straight from Heaven", almost channeling some higher power, preaching the gospel in return for their good deeds.

Emanuel Swedenborg was a Swedish inventor, author, scientist, philosopher, theologian and mystic born in 1688. When he turned 53, he started to experience strange dreams and visions. These began on the weekend of Easter in April of 1744. He believed that he was appointed by the Lord to write *The Heavenly Doctrine* in hopes to reform Christianity. His spiritual eyes were opened so that he could freely visit Heaven and Hell. His life work suddenly changed direction. He claimed he could talk to angels, demons, and other spirits. Emanuel's father who was a Professor of Theology at Uppsala University had believed that angels and spirits were present in everyday life.

Spiritual matters became a focal point for Swedenborg. His goal was to find a theory which could explain how matter relates to spirit, studying the process of creation and the structure of matter was his first steps. In Swedenborg's book *Earths in the Universe*, he stated that he spoke with spirits from Jupiter, Mars, Mercury, Saturn, Venus and the Moon. He also spoke with spirits from planets from beyond our own solar system. Swedenborg truly believed that the Bible described a human's transformation from a materialistic being to a spiritual one. He called this rebirth or regeneration. Convinced that the creation myth was the account of man's rebirth in six steps and that Jesus Christ was the example of that transformation from man to the divine.

Swedenborg published eighteen theological works which had influenced the likes of William Blake, Sir Arthur Conan Doyle, Ralph

Waldo Emerson, Hellen Keller, W.B Yeats, Immanuel Kant and Carl Jung. A religion emanated out of his teachings and philosophies. The Swedenborgian Church of America is in existence today.

Swedenborg predicted the exact date of his own death, some six months earlier, entering the spirit world for the last time on March 29th, 1772. His last words were spoken from his death bed with his hand on his heart when asked if his works were based on truth and not just to make a name for himself:

*"As truly as you see me before your eyes, so true is everything that I have written; and I could have said more had it been allowed when you enter eternity you will see everything..."*

During the process of writing this book, with the understanding that I was delving into a subject that was otherworldly, I stepped outside of my house in the middle of the night. It was one of these "pinch me" moments when I was checking my pulse. Is this for real? Am I wasting my time, spending hours upon hours of reading, researching, writing and digging into this subject? I entered into my backyard and shouted out loud, "I am ready. Show me something." Within a few seconds, I heard a faint whistling sound coming from the right side of me. It grew louder and something whizzed by and lit up for a second and then shut off. It was an orb. It was a tennis-sized ball of yellow and white light. "I am not ready!" I shouted and ran back into the house.

I have done something similar to this when I was vacationing with my family up in New Hampshire last summer. Again, during the process of writing the book, I had taken my kayak out onto Lake Winnisquam. I was solo and it was a gorgeous day. Scattered clouds, but otherwise a very clear sky above me. I was in the middle of the lake. There were a few boats scattered about, but most of the lake traffic and boats were anchored at the sandbar.

I then leaned back and looked up into the sky and said out loud, "Show me something if this is all real." Amazingly, maybe thirty seconds later, the strangest looking plane I have ever seen flew directly above me. There was no sound. It looked like it had three sets of wings. I waited for the sound to follow but it never came. I got freaked out.

I looked around. Apparently, no one was watching. No one noticed. I looked back up and continued to follow it with my eyes until it was out of sight. Then, I thought about what I had asked and the response I received. Coincidence? I quickly paddled back to the camp. I drove my kayak right into the sand of the beach and jumped out, dropping my paddles carelessly along the shore. I entered the cabin, grabbed a piece of paper and pen and began to sketch the strange-looking plane that I just witnessed.

I was sure that it was a military plane of some kind. I looked frantically online for something similar and came up empty. I did find what I think is a match of it on the thumbnail of a UFO video on Youtube.com but have been unable to locate any video of it.

Later that night, prior to fireworks at the lake, we witnessed three orange orbs follow the same path and disappear near the shore of the other side of the lake. This was July 4th weekend. Several people that we were with saw them but they assumed that they had to be Chinese lanterns. Yet again, we will automatically accept and believe that these lights in the sky are just lanterns. It is easy and it is quick. Case solved. You get on with your life. For others, they know that there is something different about those lights in the sky. The way they move, how they just appear and disappear out of nowhere. In a similar fashion, the same is assumed with Bigfoot encounters. Some witnesses describe seeing a "bear running on two legs" or a "gorilla" watching them from afar. But others will know that beyond a doubt, it was a Bigfoot. Visual sightings and physical evidence like prints can create a paradigm shift in seconds.

There have been stories of angels throughout history. As we know, there have also been stories of aliens throughout history as well. Many believe that they are one and the same. There is a mysterious race called the Annunaki. The Annunaki were the children of the gods Anu and Ki. They appeared in Babylonian myth and are mentioned in the story of Gilgamesh around the time of the great flood.

Some believe that these are the "fallen angels" who mated with "the daughters of man" creating a new type of human being. Their offspring were believed to have psychic powers and some even believed that these angel-hybrids are the forefathers of the "children of Israel". This DNA connection, it is theorized, allowed them to have a closer relationship with God through the angels. They were given protection and also were given "signs" letting them know that they were different from other humans. One of these signs was the Orange Orb.

In the book, *UFOs, Portals & Gateways,* author Nigel Mortimer describes that by the time that Moses walked the earth, the connection with the angels was in full force:

*"From time to time, they would give signs to members of their hybrid offspring, to keep the connection alive that they were different from other humans in one particular region of the planet or another. Religious texts from all over the world, indicate that amongst these 'differences' were the ability to use psychic means to make a prophecy, to understand matter and make miracles, to visit other dimensional states and visit the heavens of their 'father'. The amazingly detailed stories of Enoch, Ezekiel, and Daniel are a testament to this. Sometimes the angels would put signs in the sky for those with the psychic connection to recognize, and one of those was the hybrid Akhenaten, a contemporary of Moses in the 18th Dynasty Egypt. The Orange Balls of Light phenomena is well entrenched on the subject of modern day UFO sightings. I have experienced this kind of phenomenon myself, in fact, it was through such an experience with an OBOL in 1980 that I first became aware of the UFO reality. Thousands of years before, Akhenaten was having his own encounter with a similar if not the same phenomena."*

When Akhenaten's father had passed away he then took over the throne. Akhenaten was known for trying to abandon Egyptian polytheism by introducing worship which was centered upon the Aten. The Aten is the disk of the sun in Ancient Egyptian mythology. Akhenaten believed that the Aten was the creator, the giver of life and the nurturing spirit of the world. *"Now, it is the Orb, my father, who advised me concerning it, namely the "Horizon of the Orb"*. During his fifth year of reign, he was inspired to move his people and build them a new city in the middle of the desert. Akhenaten sighted the disk between a cleft in the cliffs at this new location. The disk spoke to his thoughts. He felt that God was speaking to him through the Aten in order for him to make a change to the land.

I spent yesterday working on the conclusion of this book. I had asked for some guidance on how I should end it. I felt like I was being told to share some information about the "Warriors of the Rainbow" prophecy. I wrote down the following quote below and then went outside to work in the yard. The sun was slowly setting. I looked up above and noticed what looked like a rainbow in the clouds. It was being created by the setting sun. Normally called a Sun Dog, they are typically seen during the winter months. The date was May 10th. The significance of "the sign" didn't hit me until the following morning. I was writing about the Warriors of the Rainbow prophecy and lo and behold there is a rainbow just above me a short time later. Not the typical rainbow arch, just a dirigible-sized band of light meshed with a cloud. It stayed there, floating above me and the yard for a good twenty minutes or so, then disappeared.

The Native American prophecy called the "Warriors of the Rainbow" tells of the keepers of legends, rituals, and other myths that will be needed when the time comes to restore Earth's health. It is believed that these legendary beings will return on a day of awakening when all people unite. Lost teachings and wisdom will resurface. What are these teachings? I believe we all have the capacity for some amazing things. I believe we all have the power of telepathy, telekinesis, premonition and the like. The paranormal was once normal. They just have been lost, tucked away. We are bombarded with distractions left and right. We have lost our way. But there is a change coming over the horizon. I can feel it.

> *"One day...there would come a time, when the earth being ravaged and polluted, the forests being destroyed, the birds would fall from the air, the waters would be blackened, the fish being poisoned in the streams, and the trees would no longer be, mankind as we would know it would all but cease to exist..."*

> *There will come a day when people of all races, colors, creeds will put aside their differences. They will come together in love, joining hands in unification, to heal the Earth and all her children. They will move over the Earth everywhere like a great Whirling Rainbow, bringing peace, understanding, and healing everywhere they go.*

> ***Many creatures thought to be extinct or mythical will resurface at this time; the great trees that perished will return almost overnight. All living things will flourish, drawing sustenance from the breath of our Mother, the Earth."***

> *The day will come, it is not far away. The day that we shall see how we owe our very existence to the people of all tribes that have maintained their culture and heritage. Those that have kept the rituals, stories, legends, and myths alive. It will be with this knowledge, the knowledge that they have preserved, that we shall once again return to 'harmony' with Nature, Mother Earth, and mankind. It will be with this knowledge that we shall find our 'Key to our Survival'".*

### - Navajo / Hopi Prophecy of the Whirling Rainbow

We all have our purpose on this planet. We all have a path. For some, their path is short and their purpose, never fulfilled. When my sister Cara passed away of cancer a few years back, at the age of 35, leaving behind two kids, it floored me, to say the least. It put all of life into perspective. We are only here for a very short period of time.

Questions bubble to the surface, the same ones that have puzzled the ancients. I continue to ask these questions, wanting to know the truth. Why am I here? Where did we come from? Where are we going? We still don't have the answers to those questions. But I do feel that what we do here on this earth will affect where we go next. And yes, I do believe in the afterlife and that we go somewhere else after this. Do we come back to live again? Repeating until we have achieved "enlightenment" or until we have found our purpose in life? Do we go to "Heaven"? Is heaven another planet, a place or another dimension? Does heaven even exist? We won't know until each of us passes through to the other side. We are all going to face the same fate.

My path has been a strange one and only I can walk it. Writing this book has been a part of my purpose in this life. Where will it lead? I don't know. I will enjoy every moment of the journey as I walk along this unknown path. With each step, more will be revealed. I have the strangest feeling that I am just getting started.

# NOTES:

CHAPTER 1 **(Monsterland, Massachusetts)**:

1.) Coleman, Loren, *Monsters of Massachusetts*, Pennsylvania. Stackpole Books. 2013. PRINT. P. 70
2.) http://www.strangeusa.com/ViewLocation.aspx?id=63947&Description=_Monsterland__Leominster__MA
3.) BFRO.net / http://bfro.net/GDB/state_listing.asp?state=ma
4.) Bartholomew, Robert E. & Bartholomew, Paul B. *Bigfoot: Encounters in New York & New England*. H. Washington, Hancock House. 2008. P. 87
5.) http://www.joshuastevens.net/visualization/squatch-watch-92-years-of-bigfoot-sightings-in-us-and-canada/
6.) Goudsward, David, *Ancient Stone Sites of New England and the Debate over early European Exploration*. North Carolina, McFarland & Company. 2006. PRINT
7.) *Interview with John E. Mack,* *http://www.pbs.org/wgbh/nova/aliens/johnmack.html*

CHAPTER 2 **(Leominster and UFOs)**:

8.) https://en.wikipedia.org/wiki/Leominster,_Massachusetts
9.) http://www.ibtimes.com/time-traveler-video-film-reveals-first-use-cell-phone-1938-video-1174407
10.) Fowler, Raymond, *The Andreasson Affa*ir, New Jersey, New Page Press, 1979, 2015. P. 215
11.) IBID
12.) Fawcett, Larry & Greenwood, Barry J. *Clear Intent: The Government Coverup of the UFO Experience*, New Jersey. Prentice Hall. 1984. P 108
13.) Fowler, Raymond, *The Watchers*, New York, Random House Publishers, 1991, p. 337
14.) Fowler, Raymond, *Anatomy of an Abductee*, p. 335
15.) IBID

16.) http://paranormal.about.com/library/blstory_november03_41. htm
17.) Fuller, John, *Incident at Exeter*, Berkley Publishing, 1978, p. 119
18.) Sanderson, Ivan T., *Invisible Residents*, Adventures Unlimited Press, 2015, p. 18
19.) Imbrogno, Phil J., *Ultraterrestrial Contact*, Llewellyn Publications, Minnesota, 2010, p. 58

Chapter 3 (**Early UFOs in Massachusetts**)

20.) Cahill, Robert Ellis, *New England's Visitors from Outer Space*, Massachusetts, Smith Publishing House. 1970. P. 14
21.) *http://www.celebrateboston.com/ufo/first-ufo-sighting.htm*
22.) Cahill, pp. 6-7
23.) IBID, p. 8

CHAPTER 4 (**Mysterious Airships of 1909**):

24.) http://www.sott.net/article/146471-Its-Raining-Fish-And-Frogs-Mysterious-falls-from-the-sky
25.) Cahill, Robert Ellis, *New England's Visitors from Outer Space*, Massachusetts, Smith Publishing House. 1970, p. 11
26.) Belanger, Jeff, *Weird Massachusetts*. New York. Sterling Publishing. 2008. P.?
27.) Keel, John A. *Operation Trojan Horse*. Texas. Anomalist Books, 2013. Pp. 117-118
28.) IBID, p. 119
29.) IBID, p. 120
30.) Providence Journal, December 24th, 1909
31.) Keel, p. 122
32.) IBID, p. 124
33.) IBID, p. 123
34.) IBID, pp. 125-126

CHAPTER 5 (**Here Come the Saucers**):

35.) Cahill, Robert Ellis, *New England's Visitors from Outer Space*, Massachusetts, Smith Publishing House. 1970, p. 14

36.) Hall, Richard H. The UFO Evidence. Washington. (National Investigations Committee on Aerial Phenomena.) 1964, p.66
37.) IBID, p. 78
38.) IBID, p. 131
39.) IBID, p. 21
40.) (https://en.wikipedia.org/wiki/1952_Washington,_D.C._UFO_in cident)
41.) Good, Timothy, *Need to Know: UFOs, the Military and Intelligence.* New York. Pegasus Books. 2007. Pp. 191
42.) IBID, p. 190
43.) IBID, p. 189
44.) IBID, p. 134
45.) IBID, p. 191
46.) Hall, Richard H. The UFO Evidence. Washington. (National Investigations Committee on Aerial Phenomena.) 1964, p. 11
47.) https://en.wikipedia.org/wiki/Barney_and_Betty_Hill
48.) Hall, Richard H. The UFO Evidence. Washington. (National Investigations Committee on Aerial Phenomena.) 1964, p. 45
49.) Cahill, Robert Ellis, *New England's Visitors from Outer Space,* Massachusetts, Smith Publishing House. 1970, p.17
50.) https://en.wikipedia.org/wiki/Northeast_blackout_of_1965
51.) Marrs, Jim, *Alien Agenda: Investigating the Extraterrestrial Presence Among Us.* Willam Morrow Paperbacks, 2000, p. 216

Chapter 6: (**The Skies are Alive**):

52.) UFO Investigator, a NICAP publication, Vol. 4, No. 5 p. 5, (March 1968) with Thanks to the Donald E. Keyhoe Archives.
53.) Hall, Richard H. The UFO Evidence. Washington. (National Investigations Committee on Aerial Phenomena.) 1964. P. 66
54.) IBID. p. 320
55.) IBID. p. 319
56.) IBID p. 330
57.) http://neufor.com/histcas3.html
58.) *http://www.ufoevidence.org/cases/case548.htm*

59.) *https://www.bostonglobe.com/metro/2015/02/23/berkshires-museum-says-alien-encounter-true/kTFw5NRfJLzax8pYD49G2N/story.html*

60.) Hall, p. 325

61.) *http://ufologie.patrickgross.org/ce3/1978-01-10-usa-southmiddleton.html*

62.) Hall p. 414

63.) IBID., p. 328

64.) IBID, p. 326

65.) IBID, p. 336

66.) IBID, p. 173

67.) IBID, p. 161

68.) IBID, p. 202

69.) Clear Intent, p. 102

70.) *The Andreasson Affair: Phase II*

71.) Hall, p. 32

Chapter 7: (**Bigfoot Tracks**)

Chapter 8: (**Who's Coming with Me?**)

72.) http://www.nature.com/news/2011/110823/full/news.2011.498.html

73.) http://bfro.net/GDB/show_report.asp?id=28017

Chapter 9: (**Paging Dr. Brake**)

74.) http://bfro.net/GDB/show_report.asp?id=28017

Chapter 10: (**Bigfoot and Leominster State Forest**)

Chapter 11: (**Bigfoot in the Bay State**)

75.) http://www.boston.com/news/local/articles/2005/10/30/tales_from_the_swamp/

76.) Bartholomew, Robert E. & Bartholomew, Paul B. *Bigfoot: Encounters in New York & New England.* H. Washington, Hancock House. 2008. P. 105

77.) IBID, p. 107

78.) IBID, p. 113
79.) http://www.bfro.net/GDB/show_report.asp?id=8717
80.) http://www.bfro.net/GDB/show_report.asp?id=6631
81.) Bartholomew, p. 69
82.) http://www.bfro.net/GDB/show_report.asp?id=1198
83.) Bartholomew, p.69-70
84.) IBID, p. 68
85.) Rife, Philip, *Bigfoot Across America,* iUniverse.com. 2000. P. 9
86.) Bartholomew, p. 123
87.) http://www.bfro.net/GDB/show_report.asp?id=26277
88.) http://www.bfro.net/GDB/show_report.asp?id=25364:

## Chapter 12: (The Orange Orbs)

89.) Fowler, Raymond, *The Andreasson Affa*ir, New Jersey, New Page Press, 1979, 2015. P. 215
90.) Fuller, John, *Incident at Exeter* p. 119
91.) Ray, Terry. *The Complete Story of the Worldwide Invasion of the Orange Orbs,* Pennsylvania, Sunberry Press. 2014. PP. 9-10
92.) https://www.youtube.com/watch?v=MDgEqnbJ8Kw
93.) Ray, Terry. P. 113
94.) Hall, Richard H. The UFO Evidence. Washington. (National Investigations Committee on Aerial Phenomena.) 1964. P. 29
95.) Ray, Terry. Pp. 9-10
96.) Ray, Terry, pp. 112-113
97.) Hall, Richard. P. 326
98.) https://www.youtube.com/watch?v=MDgEqnbJ8Kw

## Chapter 13: (Mystery Man at Miranda's)

## Chapter 14: (Is there a UFO or Bigfoot Connection?)

99.) Bord, Colin & Janet, *The Bigfoot Casebook*. Pennsylvania. Stack Pole Books, 1982 P. 74
100.) **http://www.huffingtonpost.com/dr-franklin-ruehl-phd/is-bigfoot-possibly-an-alien_b_1578844.html**

101.) Bord, Janet. *The Evidence for Bigfoot and Other Man-Beasts,* Northamptonshire, UK, 1984. P. 125

102.) Meldrum, Jeff. *Sasquatch, A Forge Paperback.* New York, 2006. P. 70

103.) http://theparanormalpastor.blogspot.com/2008/06/ufo-landing-on-presque-isle.html

104.) **http://www.examiner.com/article/sasquatch-and-ufos-and-the-high-strange-connection-interview-with-stan-gordon**

105.) Shiel, Lisa A. *Backyard Bigfoot: The True Story of Stick Signs, UFOs & Sasquatch.* Michigan. Slipdown Mountain Publications, LLC. pp. 137-138

106.) http://www.huffingtonpost.com/dr-franklin-ruehl-phd/is-bigfoot-possibly-an-alien_b_1578844.html

107.) http://ufodigest.com/article/bigfoot-ufo-1016

108.) Shield, Lisa. Pp 137-138

109.) **http://mysteriousuniverse.org/2010/09/curious-cryptohominids-a-link-between-aliens-and-bigfoot/**

**Chapter 15: (Bigfoot and the Orange Orbs)**

110.) http://bigfootevidence.blogspot.com/2015/04/these-strange-lights-have-been-reported.html

111.) Imbrogno, Philip. *Celtic Mysteries of New England,* Minnesota, Llewellyn Publications.    2000. P. 108

112.) Burnette, Tom & Rob Riggs, *Bigfoot: Exploring the Myth and Discovering the Truth*

113.) IBID, p. 110

114.) Shiel, Lisa A., *Forbidden Bigfoot*, Jacobsville Books, 2013

115.) Burnette, Tom & Rob Riggs, p. 229

116.) Bord, Janet, *Evidence for Bigfoot and Other Man-Beasts*, p. 125

117.) Bord, Colin & Janet, p. 84

118.) Shiel, Lisa A. *Backyard Bigfoot*, p. 137

119.) https://www.theguardian.com/science/2014/may/18/matter-light-photons-electrons-positrons

120.) Burnette, Tom & Rob Riggs, p. 178

121.) https://jbullfrog74.wordpress.com/2009/04/13/khat-hansen-interview/

122.) Imbrogno, Philip A. Interdimensional Universe, p. 169

Chapter 16: (**Interdimensional Bigfoot**)

123.) Imbrogno, Philip A. *Files from the Edge*, Llewellyn Publications, Minnesota, 2010, p.177

http://disinfo.com/2013/10/sasquatch-seatco-indians-conversation-henry-franzoni/

124.) http://paranormalistics.blogspot.com/p/what-is-bigfoot.html
125.) http://paranormalistics.blogspot.com/p/what-is-bigfoot.html
126.) Lasperitis, Kewaunee, *The Psychic Sasquatch and their UFO Connection*, Createspace,     2005, p. 32
127.) IBID, p. 6
128.) IBID, p. 12
129.) Bord, Colin & Janet, pp. 115-116
130.) Lasperitis, Kewaunee, *The Psychic Sasquatch*, p. 1
131.) Bord, Colin & Janet, p. 156
132.) *http://www.crystalinks.com/hsii.html*

Chapter 17: (**Marbles from the Other Side**)

133.) https://www.youtube.com/watch?v=O2OCE4etCZA

Chapter 18: (**Is Leominster State Forest a Sacred Place?**)

134.) https://en.wikipedia.org/wiki/Lancaster,_Massachusetts
135.) Emerson, William A. *Leominster Traditions*, 1891
136.) http://www.journey2theheart.com/akashicrecords.htm
137.) Goudsward, David, *Ancient Stone Sites of New England and the Debate over early European Exploration*. North Carolina, McFarland & Company. 2006. P. 159
138.) Worcester Telegram and Gazette, July 1974
139.) Goudsward, David, p. 14
140.) Imbrogno, Philip A. Celtic Mysteries, p. 66
141.) IBID, p. 97
142.) IBID, p. 14
143.) IBID, p. 15
144.) Burnette, Tom & Rob Riggs, p. 181
145.) Imbrogno, p. 4
146.) IBID, p. 123
147.) IBID, p. 181

148.) IBID, p. 105

149.) IBID, p. 112

150.) Keel, John, *Operation Trojan Horse*, p. 169

151.) Bradshaw, Linda & Tom Dongo, *Merging Dimensions*, Light Technology Publications, Arizona, 1995, p. 75

152.) Belanger, Jeff, *Weird New England*, p. 72

153.) Keel, John, *Mysterious Beings*

154.) http://www.iflscience.com/environment/what-caused-china-s-floating-city-sky

155.) https://www.nasa.gov/mission_pages/sunearth/news/mag-portals.html

156.) https://en.m.wikipedia.org/wiki/Fata_Morgana_(mirage)

157.) https://en.m.wikipedia.org/wiki/Fata_Morgana_(mirage)

158.) http://www.express.co.uk/news/science/612531/Did-parallel-universe-open-up-Hundreds-see-floating-city-filmed-in-skies-above-China

159.) http://www.express.co.uk/news/world/565315/Scientists-at-Large-Hadron-Collider-hope-to-make-contact-with-PARALLEL-UNIVERSE-in-days

160.) https://www.youtube.com/watch?v=yeNI-kF7pSU&app=desktop

# BIBLIOGRAPHY:

Bartholomew, Robert E. & Bartholomew, Paul B. *Bigfoot: Encounters in New York & New England.* H. Washington, Hancock House. 2008.

Belanger, Jeff: *Weird Massachusetts,* Sterling Publishing, India, 2008

Bord, Janet and Colin, *Bigfoot Casebook Updated: Sightings and Encounters from 1818 to 2004,* Pine Winds Press, 1982 & 2006

Bord, Janet and Colin, *The Evidence for Bigfoot and other Man-Beasts,* Wellingborough, Northamptonshire, The Aquarian Press, .1984

Bradshaw, Linda & Tom Dongo, *Merging Dimensions,* Light Technology Publications, Arizona, 1995

Burnette, Tom & Rob Riggs, Bigfoot: *Exploring the Myth and Discovering the Truth,* Llewellyn Publications, 2014

Cahill, Robert Ellis, *New England's Visitors from Outer Space,* Massachusetts, Smith Publishing House. 1970

Coleman, Loren: *Monsters of Massachusetts,* Stackpole Books, Pennsylvania, 2013

Coleman, Loren: *Mysterious America,* New York, New York, Paraview, 2001, 2007

Dewhurst, Richard J., *The Ancient Giants who ruled America,* Bear and Company, Rochester, Vermont

Emerson, William A., *Leominster Traditions,* 1891

Fawcett, Larry & Greenwood, Barry J. *Clear Intent: The Government Coverup of the UFO Experience,* New Jersey. Prentice Hall. 1984

Fowler, Raymond E., *The Andreasson Affair*, Englewood Cliffs, Prentice-Hall, 1979

Fowler, Raymond E., *The Watchers*, New York, New York, Bantam Books, 1990

Fowler, Raymond E. UFO Testament: Anatomy of an Abductee, iUniverse, 2012

Fuller, John, *Incident at Exeter*, Berkley Publishing, 1978

Goudsward, David, *Ancient Stone Sites of New England and the Debate over early European Exploration*. North Carolina, McFarland & Company. 2006

Hall, Richard H. *The UFO Evidence*. Washington. (National Investigations Committee on Aerial Phenomena.) 1964

Imbrogno, Philip. *Celtic Mysteries of New England*, Minnesota, Llewellyn Publications.    2000.

Imbrogno, Philip A. *Files from the Edge*, Llewellyn Publications, Minnesota, 2010

Imbrogno, Philip A. *Interdimensional Universe*, Llewellyn Publications, Minnesota, 2008

Imbrogno, Phil J., *Ultraterrestrial Contact*, Llewellyn Publications, Minnesota,

Good, Timothy, *Need to Know: UFOs, the Military and Intelligence*. New York. Pegasus Books. 2007

Keel, John, *The Complete Guide to Mysterious Beings*, Amazon Digital Services, 2014

Keel, John A. *Operation Trojan Horse*. Texas. Anomalist Books, 2013.

Lasperitis, Kewaunee, The Psychic Sasquatch and their UFO Connection, Createspace, 2005

Marrs, Jim, *Alien Agenda: Investigating the Extraterrestrial Presence Among Us*. Willam Morrow Paperbacks, 2000

McLeod, Michael, *Anatomy of a Beast: Obsession and myth on the trail of Bigfoot*, Berkley, California, University of California Press, 2009

Meldrum, Dr. Jeff, *Sasquatch: Legend Meets Science,* New York, New York, Tom Doherty Associates, 2006

Napier, John, Bigfoot: *The Yeti, Sasquatch in Myth and Reality,* New York, New York, E.P. Dutton & Company, Inc. 1973

Pace, Marian T., *Bigfoot: All Over the Country*, New York, New York, Dodd, Mead & Company, 1978

Ray, Terry. *The Complete Story of the Worldwide Invasion of the Orange Orbs,* Pennsylvania, Sunberry Press. 2014.

Rife, Philip, *Bigfoot Across America,* iUniverse.com. 2000

Sanderson, Ivan T., *Invisible Residents*, Adventures Unlimited Press,

Shiel, Lisa A. *Backyard Bigfoot: The True Story of Stick Signs, UFOs & Sasquatch*. Michigan. Slipdown Mountain Publications, LLC. 2005

Shiel, Lisa A., *Forbidden Bigfoot*, Jacobsville Books, 2013

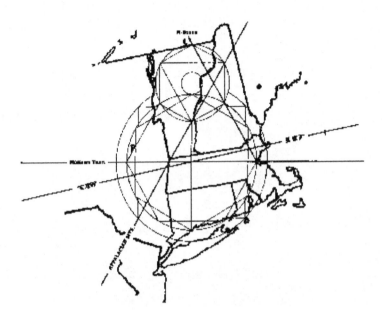

Massachusetts Ley Lines - Courtesy of www.starseedbobs.blogspot.com

Author Ronny Le Blanc - Matt Moneymaker founder of BFRO

**THE MONSTERLAND PODCAST – Launched 2017**

 Monsterland: Encounters with UFOs, Bigfoot and
Orange Orbs shared a link.
October 31 at 2:31pm · 🌐

Local author pens tales of Leominster's 'Monsterland'
LEOMINSTER -- Growing up in Leominster, Ronny LeBlanc never questioned where
the name "Monsterland" came from.

SENTINELANDENTERPRISE.COM

**Sentinel and Enterprise Front Page - Halloween 10.31.16**

Courtesy of Mike Paterson – Bigfoot Trackway – Canada

Courtesy of Mike Paterson – Bigfoot Track – Single Print – Canada

Author's Photo - White Orb - Leominster, MA

GREATER NEW ENGLAND UFO CONFERENCE

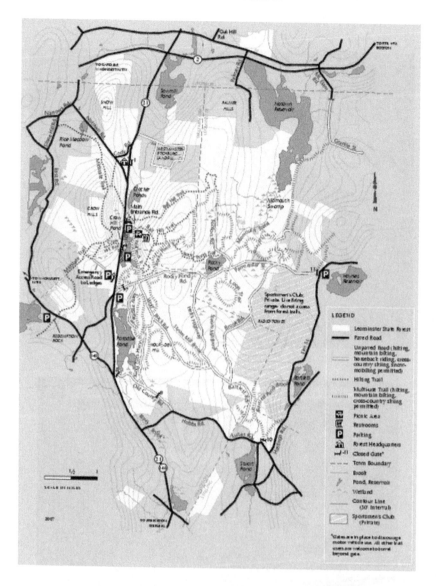

# LEOMINSTER STATE FOREST TRAIL MAP

# ABOUT THE AUTHOR

Ronny Le Blanc graduated from Vanguard University in Southern California with a Communications Degree specializing in Film and Television Production. He currently works as the Vice President of Sales and Business Development for a Boutique Advertising Agency outside of Boston. He is married with four children and currently resides in Leominster, Massachusetts.

## www.RonnyLeBlanc.com

"IF YOU WANT TO FIND THE SECRETS OF THE UNIVERSE, THINK IN TERMS OF ENERGY, FREQUENCY, AND VIBRATION."

### NIKOLA TESLA

CPSIA information can be obtained
at www.ICGtesting.com
Printed in the USA
BVOW06s0124271017

498807BV00021B/148/P

9 780692 652374